THE LITTLE GOURMET

Cookbook for Children

By
ROSALIE RIVERA

AUTHOR

Rosalie Rivera
Cooking Teacher and Culinary Consultant
Auxiliary Board Member, The Children's Hospital of Philadelphia

(Section on chocolate by Judy Worrell; Auxiliary member, The Children's Hospital of Philadelphia; Pet recipes by Ann Hess, Veterinary Department, Philadelphia Zoological Gardens; Ned Moser, M.S., V.M.D., School of Veterinary Medicine, University of Pennsylvania; Sheldon L. Gerstenfeld, V.M.D., Chestnut Hill Veterinary Hospital, Bird Clinic; and Barbara Toddes, Animal Nutritionist, the Philadelphia Zoological Gardens)

EDITING

Rosalie Rivera
Editorial assistance by the Public Relations Department
of The Children's Hospital of Philadelphia

Cover art by Vicki Fox
Inside illustrations by Kimberly Rivera, age 14

Library of Congress Catalog Card Number:
86-61865

International Standard Book Number 0-9617370-0-X

Supported by a grant from the Saga Corporation of Menlo Park, California.

ACKNOWLEDGEMENTS

As I was writing this cookbook, it became clear that there were many special people who made this cookbook a reality.

I would like to express my sincere appreciation to the Saga Corporation for its generosity in underwriting the cost of publishing the cookbook.

Edna Wallace, Andrea Price and Beverly Epstein have devoted countless hours to this cookbook. They have given me the benefit of their knowledge and expertise as this project grew from the talking stage to the publishing stage. I value not only their professionalism but also their friendship and support.

My thanks and appreciation to the Auxiliary of The Children's Hospital of Philadelphia, its President, Teddy Manero, and the Auxiliary staff liaison, Chris Murphy.

Without Vicki Fox, there would not be a cover for the cookbook. A very gifted artist, she has captured the feeling of the cookbook with her wonderful cover illustration.

The Testing Committee included many parents and children who tested many of these recipes in their home kitchens and rated them according to their appeal and skill level. I would like to thank Mrs. Sandy Avender, along with Denise, Age 10 and Lauren, Age 7; Mrs. Jane DiLella and Dan Jr., Age 12; Mrs. Ellen Gasiewski with Margaret, Age 8, Tom, Age 10 and Dan, Age 12; Mrs. Eileen Kettrick with Heather, Age 13; Mrs. Ella Lindenhofen with David, Age 8, Jason, Age 12; Mrs. Trish Lunardi, along with Kathi, Age 14 and Mark, Age 15; Mrs. Anne McCabe and Alice, Age 10; Mrs. Joan Prendergast, along with Katie, Age 12, Megan, Age 10, Julie, Age 13 and Denise, Age 5. Thanks also to Mrs. Andrea Price along with Chris, Age 9, Andrew, Age 11 and David, Age 13; Mrs. Janet Stewart and Daniel, Age 5 and Elisabeth, Age 1, who tasted each recipe; Mrs. Catherine Tascione along with Caroline, Age 6, Nicky, Age 9, and Bernadette, Age 12. I also wish to thank Mrs. Rita Jackson, Mrs. Terry Hirshorn, Mrs. Sondra Sokel and Mrs. Kathy Rosse for their contributions to the cookbook.

A special thanks to Judy Worrell who contributed many of the chocolate recipes and tested them with her children, Caroline, Age 13 and Fred, Age 14.

3

ACKNOWLEDGEMENTS (continued)

To Marcy Makadon who suggested that children would love to have recipes for their pets. A thank you also to Dr. Sheldon L. Gerstenfeld, Barbara Toddes, Animal Nutritionist, and Dr. Ned Moser for the animal treat recipes.

I am also indebted to Shirley Bonnem, Vice-President of Public Relations and Development at The Children's Hospital of Philadelphia, who believed from the beginning that this cookbook could be a joy for both parents and children.

And finally to Orlando, Kimberly and Alexander Rivera who have been my toughest critics and my most appreciative audience.

Thank you all.

INTRODUCTION

Children love to cook. In earlier days, mom or grandmom was there in the kitchen with wonderful smells of homemade soup, streudel or fresh pies. Little ones were encouraged to taste and help out under loving supervision. At the same time, problems were discussed, wisdom gained and family communication strengthened. The dinner table brought everyone together to share events of the day and enjoy the meal and the company.

Lifestyles change and roles change. Dinner time is sometimes fast food takeout, or very late because both parents work. Some parents love to cook but don't have the time or patience for a child in the kitchen. Others do not enjoy cooking because their parents never made them feel relaxed or confident in cooking. But all of us share the wish that our children, both boys and girls alike, have a good food experience.

Here are a few suggestions which I recommend in working with children in the kitchen:

- Choose a mutually convenient time and discuss priorities. There may be shopping to do. How long will this project take? Are you ready to clean up after you're done? All these things are important.

- Read through the recipe first and see if it interests you, or should you make it for another member of the family who happens to love "Chocolatines"?

- Get all your ingredients out before you start. Do you need to chop or mince or peel any of the ingredients listed in the recipe before you begin?

- Parents should be there to assist, answer questions and provide help if needed, but resist the urge to take over. Be patient.

- Praise success, however minor. Minimize failures and don't expect perfection. We all learn by our mistakes. When children put in 2 Tablespoons of salt instead of 2 Tablespoons of sugar, they will remember to read instructions more carefully after the first bite.

- Parents should try to arrange to take their children on field trips. Try farmers' markets, a seafood store, the butcher, a dairy farm, strawberry picking, a bakery tour or even Aunt Emma's vegetable garden can be a treat.

5

- Children need to know what fresh produce looks like. How can you tell a fresh fish? How do you compare prices? Why is it important to read the ingredients on labels or the back of boxes?

The "Little Gourmet" was written as a learning tool for child, novice cook or anyone who finds cooking or baking mysterious. Cooking and baking can be an art form, and children of varied abilities can express themselves in a very personal way. It creates a good self-image and a true sense of accomplishment. They will build on this skill through adulthood.

We hope you enjoy working with "The Little Gourmet."

CONTENTS

ACKNOWLEDGEMENTS

INTRODUCTION

Kitchen

Safety

KITCHEN SAFETY

Remember when you first learned to ride your bike, there were certain rules and regulations you had to follow in order to be safe. It is exactly the same way in the kitchen. There are certain things that can go wrong that can cause you harm. With a few precautions and knowledge, you will enjoy many wonderful <u>safe</u> hours in your kitchen.

Check first with mom or dad (or another adult in the house) to see if you have permission to work in the kitchen and if they will be there to give you some guidance. Here are a few tips:

(1) HANDS - Wash your hands with lots of soap and hot water before you get started. Dirt and germs on your hands can be transferred to food and can make someone very ill, so make sure they are sparkling clean.

(2) CLOTHES - Do not wear large shirts or blouses that might catch fire. Tie back long hair which could also catch fire or fall into food. Remove any large bracelets that could catch on a pot handle and spill boiling water.

(3) APPLIANCES - Never touch switches or plugs with wet hands. Be very careful with sharp blades on blenders or food processors. Make sure their covers are in place before starting. Check with an adult to see if you are permitted to use an appliance. Waffle irons are very hot even after they have been unplugged for 5 or 10 minutes.

(4) FLAMMABLE ARTICLES - Dish towels, pot holders, paper recipes and cookbooks can catch fire in a second. Keep them far away from the flame.

(5) HEAT - Do not pick up a hot pot with a wet towel or wet pot holder. The heat will go right through and burn you. Turn pot handles away from the edge of the stove. Watch for toddlers in the kitchen that might pull over a hot pot or pick up a sharp knife. Direct them out of the kitchen while you are cooking. Do not put a hot glass plate that has been in the oven directly onto a cold counter. The glass will shatter and crack because of the quick change in temperature. Your recipe will have to be thrown out because of the danger of unseen glass in the food. You can also give yourself a bad burn if you are holding onto the plate at the time it cracks.

KITCHEN SAFETY (continued)

(6) GREASE FIRES -

Rule No. 1 - Children should never be alone in the kitchen when using the stove or an oven. There should be adult supervision at all times.

Rule No. 2 - In case of a grease fire, the supervising adult should never throw water on the fire. The adult should turn off the stove or oven, stand back, get everyone out of the kitchen and either throw baking soda (which is not caked) at the base of the flame, or use a fire extinguisher. Fire extinguishers should be checked periodically to see if they are full and in proper working order. Placing a lid on a pot will also work by cutting off the air supply to the fire. The phone number of the local fire department should be taped to the telephone. Parents should discuss with their children how to get out of the house in case of fire, where to meet and what to do. A practice fire drill is very important.

AS A MATTER OF INTEREST, if children are alone in their own home or a friend's home when a fire starts, they should not attempt to put it out. They should quickly leave the house and close any doors behind them to confine the fire to that room or area. They should get to a phone immediately, dial the fire department and give the exact address of the house where the fire is located.

(7) GLASS - It is best for children to work with utensils which are either plastic or stainless steel. Glass can become slippery for little sticky, wet hands.

(8) KNIVES - Check with an adult as to what knife you may use and what you are going to cut. That person may wish to help you if there is a chance the knife could slip or the task is too difficult for your age. An adult might also offer some techniques with the use of the knife. A dull knife is always more dangerous than a sharp knife.

(9) GARBAGE DISPOSALS - If you accidentally drop a spoon or fork into the garbage disposal, WAIT. Make sure it is off first. Ask an adult to retrieve it for you. Older children may do this with great caution.

(10) TRASH - Never go searching through the trash for a lost item. The sharp tops of lids or broken glass may cause a nasty cut. Get some help.

11

KITCHEN SAFETY (continued)

(11) STEAM AND BOILING WATER - Lift lid openings away from you and be careful sliding, not dropping, food into boiling water. It can splash up and give you a bad burn.

(12) UTENSILS - Look at your pots and pans carefully to see which ones have wooden handles. Use these for the stove as they do not get as hot as copper or aluminum handles. Use two pot holders to pick up a hot pot. Use one for the handle and the other to balance the other side of the pan. When using a vegetable peeler, peel away from you. A young child peeling a carrot or potato can use a rubber band in the center to mark the middle. First do one side and then the other. There is little chance of getting nicked.

(13) RUSHING - Most accidents happen when people are in a hurry and are less careful. Cook or bake when you are relaxed and have the time. Always think about what you are doing.

(14) FALLS - Do not try to climb on counters to reach high cabinets. Use a sturdy stepstool or get an adult to reach for you. Never reach over a stove. If you mop the kitchen floor when you are cleaning up, put a chair or two in front so people know it is wet and slippery. A little note taped on the chair would be even better.

(15) CLEAN-UP - If you are going to cook or bake, you are going to have to take the responsibility to clean up also. All utensils and surfaces should be washed well with soap and hot water to prevent disease. Don't forget to clean your cutting board.

If you can think of any other hazards in your kitchen, write them down in this book. Then you will always remember them.

Accidents are usually unpredictable, but if you know beforehand how they can be avoided, you will have a safer and happier experience in the kitchen.

Now you are ready to get started.

Nutrition

NUTRITION

A JUNIOR GUIDE TO GOOD HEALTH

While you are learning to cook, it is necessary to learn how to balance your diet or the food you eat.

Your daily food requirements should include food from the following food groups:

VEGETABLE-FRUIT GROUP (Vitamins A and C and fiber)

Include 4 servings daily.

   Suggestions:

   Dark green and deep yellow vegetables such as spinach, kale, broccoli, sweet potatoes or carrots. Citrus fruits such as oranges, grapefruit, tangerines and lemons are full of vitamin C. Other good sources are melons, berries and tomatoes.

BREAD-CEREAL GROUP (Carbohydrates, Thiamin [B_1], Iron and Niacin)

Include 3 to 4 servings daily.
   Suggestions:

   Enriched or whole-grain breads and cereals.
   Avoid sugar-coated cereals.

MILK-CHEESE GROUP (Calcium, Riboflavin [B_2] and Protein)

Children under 9	2 to 3 servings
Children 9 to 12	3 servings
Teens	4 servings

   Suggestions:

   Whole, skim, lowfat, evaporated, and nonfat dry milk, buttermilk, yogurt, ice cream, ice milk, cheese and cottage cheese.

MEAT GROUP (Protein, Niacin, Iron and Thiamin [B_1])

   Meat/Poultry/Fish/Beans
Include 2 servings daily.
   Suggestions:

   Lean beef, veal, lamb, pork, chicken, turkey, fish, shellfish (crabs, scallops, shrimp, oysters), liver, dried beans, peas, eggs, seeds, nuts and peanut butter.

NUTRITION

OTHER FOOD GROUP (Carbohydrates and Fats)

No serving size is suggested but should be determined by individual caloric needs. Less calories are needed if you would like to lose weight and more calories are needed if you wish to gain weight. Calories are a measure of the energy food provides. The extra calories that you get and your body does not use up are stored as fat.

Includes:

Butter, margarine, oil, catsup, mustard, pancake syrup, sugar, jams, jellies and soft drinks.

Here are a few nutritional suggestions that will help you work and play better:

EAT LESS SUGAR

Sugar adds calories which can make you gain weight. It also causes cavities. Between meal snacks with sugar are worse than sugar within the meal. Brush your teeth after eating sweet or sticky foods. Eat less candy, cookies, pastries, fruits canned in heavy syrup and sweetened cereals.

Think about the last time you ate a whole chocolate bar. You had energy immediately but in a short time you were tired and maybe a little sad. The reason for this strange occurrence is caffeine and the amount of sugar in chocolate. It is not good for you in large quantities. It is also not good for your teeth. (Note: Coffee, tea and cola drinks also have caffeine.)

A nice cold apple or a sweet peach would give you energy and be very satisfying. They will not add an ounce to your waist, unless you eat several.

The key to good nutrition is moderation. So be careful about the amount of sweets you consume.

EAT LESS FAT

Fats add to the level of cholesterol in the body which increases the chance of heart disease. Fat also is the largest source of calories. Trim fat off meats carefully and eat more fruits, vegetables, breads and whole-grain cereals. Cut down on red meats and eat more fish and poultry. Limit the amount of nuts and peanut butter. Use skim or low fat milk.

NUTRITION

EAT LESS SALT

Too much salt (sodium) can lead to high blood pressure and to strokes. Limit your use of the salt shaker to cooking, and then in small amounts. Try not to use the salt shaker at the table to reseason food. Watch out for hidden salt in ham, lunch meats, smoked fish, sardines, potato chips, pretzels, pickles and salted popcorn.

EAT MORE FIBER

Fiber adds bulk to your diet and not only helps prevent constipation but may also help you lose weight as bulky foods fill you up quickly. Fiber foods include whole grain breads and cereals, bran, dried peas, beans, nuts, fruits and vegetables.

Also, drink plenty of fluids, including water.

You are what you eat.

Table

Etiquette

KLM

TABLE ETIQUETTE FOR CHILDREN

It is not necessary to wear white gloves and sit in your seat like a soldier to have proper table etiquette. It is necessary, though, to have consideration for other people and their feelings.

Each meal should be a small celebration when family members relax together and talk about the plans for the day or what has already happened in their day. It is a time when everyone should feel important and special.

Here are a few pointers to help you develop manners which will make you welcome at any dinner table:

- Arrive on time for all meals.
- If you are delayed for any emergency, call and advise.
- Spruce up by washing your hands and face and brushing your hair.
- Ask the cook if you can help with last minute preparations or set the table (diagram attached).
- Wait for everyone, including the cook, to be seated before you begin to pass the food or begin to eat.
- Keep the conversation friendly. Keep major problems or complaints until another time.
- Television should be off. Find a calm station on the radio.
- Tell your friends not to call during meal times.
- Keep your napkin in your lap for wipes or spills.
- Keep family pets out of the dining room if they tend to beg for food.
- Eat with your mouth closed especially if you have braces.
- Do not talk with food in your mouth.
- Let one person talk at a time. You will have your turn but be patient.
- If you absolutely hate something on your plate, just say "not tonight, please." You do not want to hurt the cook's feelings. Remember to show the cook respect and be gracious. It really doesn't hurt to try something new. You may be surprised and find a reward of a great dessert that is hiding in the kitchen. Only the chef knows.
- When you are done, ask to be excused and take your plate and utensils into the kitchen.

<u>TABLE ETIQUETTE FOR CHILDREN</u> (continued)

- When company comes for dinner, sit quietly and wait for them to finish before you leave the table.
- If you are dining at a friend's home, thank the host or hostess for inviting you.

Can you think of any more?

If you can remember all of the above, you are pretty terrific and will make your family and friends very happy.

But don't forget, a dirty kitchen is a lonely place. Stop in and lend a hand to the cook, whoever that may be (mom or dad, grandmom or Uncle Bill). Some of the best private times happen between a parent and child when they are drying dishes. Take advantage of these moments.

COOKING TERMS AND TECHNIQUES

BAKE	To cook by dry heat in the oven. Always preheat the oven for 10 or 15 minutes before using.
BARBECUE	To cook on a grill over intense heat. You can barbecue with wood, charcoal or on a gas grill.
BASTE	To moisten food while cooking. This adds flavor and keeps food from drying out.
BEAT	To mix quickly and thoroughly in order to make a mixture smooth and light by using a fork, spoon, wire whisk, egg beater or electric beater.
BLEND	To stir, rather than beat, ingredients until they are thoroughly combined.
BOIL	To heat a liquid until bubbles break continually on the surface.
BRAISE	To cook slowly, usually covered, in a little liquid or fat.
BROIL	To cook under direct heat under a flame or heating unit.
BROWN	To cook until very light brown in color by cooking quickly in hot fat on top of the stove or at a high temperature in the oven or broiler.
CHILL	To refrigerate until cold.
CHOP	To cut solids into small pieces with a knife.
CLARIFY	To make a substance pure or clear.
COOL	To let hot food sit at room temperature until it is no longer hot.
CREAM	To beat into a creamy consistency. An example is butter and sugar.
CRIMP	Pinching the edges of a pie crust to make a decorative edge or seal the edges of a 2-crust pie.
CURE	To preserve by drying and salting and/or smoking.
CUT IN	To blend shortening into flour with a pastry blender or 2 knives used scissor-fashion until it resembles coarse crumbs.
DICE	To cut into small cubes.
DREDGE	To cover solid food with sugar, flour or other dry ingredients.
FILLET	To remove the bones from meat or fish.
FLOUR	To sprinkle lightly with flour.

22

Cooking Terms and Techniques…(continued)

FOLD	To mix an ingredient gently by passing a spoon or spatula down through the middle of the mixture, across the bottom and up to the top until it is well combined but has maintained air and volume.
FRY	To cook in hot fat.
GARNISH	To add a decorative touch to food with the addition of parsley, a slice of lemon, vegetables or olives, before serving.
GRATE	To reduce food to small pieces by rubbing it on the teeth of a grater.
GREASE	To rub a dish or pan with fat so food does not stick.
GRILL	To broil on a gridiron over hot coals or under a hot broiler.
JULIENNE	To cut into thin strips.
MARINATE	To cover food in a flavorful liquid to tenderize and render the food more flavorful. An acid, such as wine, lemon or vinegar is necessary to break down fibers and make the food more tender.
MINCE	To chop very fine.
MIX	To combine 2 or more ingredients.
MOUSSE	A delicate mixture containing whipped cream or beaten egg whites.
PEEL	To remove the peels from vegetables or fruit.
PINCH	A small amount that you can hold between your thumb and forefinger.
POACH	To simmer gently in a liquid.
PREHEAT	To heat an oven or broiler to a certain temperature before using.
PUREE	To mash food to a thick, smooth pulp.
ROAST	To cook by dry heat in an oven.
ROUX	A mixture of melted fat and flour. This is a common thickening agent in sauces and soups.
SAUTE	To cook food briefly in a small amount of hot fat.
SEASON	To add salt, pepper, spices or herbs to increase the flavor of food.
SIMMER	To cook a liquid at a low heat just below the boiling point.
STEAM	To cook by means of vapor from boiling liquid rising through the food.
STIR	To mix food with a spoon or fork using a circular motion.

STOCK	The liquid produced by slow cooking meat, poultry, fish, bones or vegetables and used as a basis for soups, sauces and gravies.
THAW	To remove food from the freezer until it is no longer frozen. It is best to thaw food in the refrigerator overnight so it defrosts slowly yet remains cold.
WHIP	To lighten and increase the volume by beating.
WHISK	To beat quickly with a whisk or whip until well blended.

BAKING TERMS AND TECHNIQUES

BAKE	To cook in an oven with dry heat.
BATTER	A beaten mixture of flour, liquid and other ingredients such as milk or eggs, and usually thin enough to pour.
BEAT	To mix rapidly with a whisk, a spoon, an electric mixer or a hand-held rotary mixer.
BLEND	To stir ingredients until they are thoroughly combined.
CREAM	To beat or rub a fat and a dry ingredient together. When you cream butter and sugar together for a cake, they will become lighter in color and will not look sugary or greasy when creamed sufficiently.
CRUST	The outer or under surface of bread, pie or pie crust.
DUST	To lightly cover a surface with flour, sugar or nuts.
FOLD	Gently blending 2 or more ingredients by turning one part over the other with a spatula, an electric mixer or by hand. Go down to the bottom through the middle, then across the bottom and bring up some batter over the top of the mixture and repeat until blended. Egg whites folded into a chocolate mousse base will be beautiful and light.
GREASE	To spread a cookie sheet or pan with fat or shortening. This prevents your recipe from sticking.
KNEAD	To mix and work a mixture into a uniform mass by pressing and pulling with the hand. The mixture will become smooth and elastic. To knead bread, press down and push with the heel of one or both hands, rotate a little, then fold over and press down again. The newer models of electric mixers now come with dough hooks which make kneading easy.

24

BAKING TERMS AND TECHNIQUES (continued)

LEAVENING — The production of gas in a batter or dough to cause it to rise. Leavening agents include baking soda, baking powder and yeast. The consistency of the dough becomes lighter and more digestible.

MOUSSE — A mousse is a very delicate mixture containing whipped cream or beaten egg whites. We often think of a light and airy lemon, chocolate or strawberry mousse, but mousses can also have pureed meat, fish or vegetable bases which are strengthened with the addition of gelatin and are served cold.

PREHEAT — To preheat means to raise the temperature of the oven or broiler to the desired setting before use. A recipe will never work correctly if you put it into a cold oven.

SIFT — To pass through a sieve or sifter in order to make dry ingredients lighter (example: flour) and remove any coarse particles. One cup of unsifted flour has more flour than 1 cup of sifted flour, so watch your recipe.

SOUFFLE — A souffle is a hot fluffy preparation made from a flavorful base to which stiffly beaten egg whites have been added. It must be eaten as soon as it is taken from the oven. It will collapse and fall after about 15 or 20 minutes, but it will still be delicious.

STIR — Stirring is the process of rotating a spoon in a bowl until the ingredients are combined. If you are too rough, then this is called "beating" and you will ruin such recipes as good muffins or a light cake or cookie. Always take your time.

WHIP — Beating eggs or heavy cream until they are thick and fluffy as you incorporate air.

WHISK — To beat with quick, light movements with a wire whisk or whip until blended.

BASIC COOKING AND BAKING EQUIPMENT

Most of the equipment that you will need is already in your kitchen. For your information, we have listed some of this equipment according to the job it does:

MEASURING

Measuring Spoons — A set - ¼, ½, 1 teaspoon and 1 Tablespoon sizes.
Plastic Measuring Cups — A set - ¼, ⅓, ½ and 1 cup sizes.
(Note: Use a knife to level off measuring spoons or cups.)
Ruler
Meat Thermometer
Oven Thermometer
Timer

MIXING

Rotary Hand Beater
Electric Mixer
Wire Whisk
Wooden Spoons or Spatula

COOKING

Various Pots and Pans
    (Discuss with parents what pans and sizes will work best with your recipes)
Saucepans
Frying Pans
Saute Pan
Large Kettle with Cover
Loaf Pan
Roasting Pan
Casseroles

BAKING

Round Cake Pans
Rectangular Cake Pans
Wire Cooling Racks
Pie Pans
Baking Sheet
Muffin Pan
Rolling Pin
Flour Sifter
Pastry Blender
Pastry Brush

CUTTING AND CHOPPING

Paring Knife
Chopping Knife
A Cook's Knife suitable for your age and ability.
Grater
Chopping Board
Food Processor
Vegetable Peeler

MISCELLANEOUS

Pot Holders
Can Opener
Slotted Spoon
Colander
Sieve
Bulb Baster
Metal Tongs
Juicer
Pancake Turner
Apple Corer
Zester
Pepper Grinder
Funnel
Kitchen Shears
Pastry Bag
Cookie Cutters

FOOD STORAGE

Plastic Wrap
Aluminum Foil
Waxed Paper
Plastic Bags
Plastic Storage Containers in various sizes.

Note: The most important food storage appliance is your refrigerator. Make sure all perishable food is refrigerated properly. Leftover food must go into the refrigerator quickly to avoid spoilage. You can never be too careful.

USEFUL BUT NOT ESSENTIAL ITEMS

Waffle Iron
Electric Deep-Fat Fryer
Electric Ice Cream Machine
Crock Pot

MEASUREMENTS AND EQUIVALENTS

3 teaspoons	=	1 Tablespoon		
4 Tablespoons	=	¼ cup		
8 Tablespoons	=	½ cup		
1 cup	=	½ pint	=	8 ounces
2 cups	=	1 pint	=	16 ounces (1 pound)
4 cups	=	2 pints or 1 quart	=	32 ounces
6 cups	=	1½ quarts		
8 cups	=	2 quarts		
4 quarts	=	1 gallon		
16 ounces	=	1 pound		

Butter Equivalents

1 Tablespoon	=	⅛ stick	=	½ ounce
2 Tablespoons	=	¼ stick	=	1 ounce
4 Tablespoons (¼ cup)	=	½ stick	=	2 ounces
8 Tablespoons (½ cup)	=	1 stick	=	4 ounces (¼ pound)
16 Tablespoons (1 cup)	=	2 sticks	=	8 ounces (½ pound)
32 Tablespoons (2 cups)	=	4 sticks	=	16 ounces (1 pound)

Other

Brown Sugar	1 pound	=	2⅓ cups
Confectioners Sugar	1 pound	=	4 cups
Egg Whites, U.S. large	1 White	=	2 Tablespoons
	8 Whites	=	1 cup
Egg Yolks, U.S. large	1 Yolk	=	1 Tablespoon
	16 Yolks	=	1 cup

A Garden In
Your Kitchen

A GARDEN IN YOUR KITCHEN

You can create wonderful plants on your kitchen windowsill with avocado pits, carrot tops or lima beans. Here are a few suggestions to get you started, but don't forget to feel the soil every once in a while to see whether the plant needs water. If it is too damp, don't water. Only water your plants when the soil feels dry or when the plant leaves look droopy.

1. **LEMON, GRAPEFRUIT and ORANGE SEEDS**

   Poke a few small holes in the bottom of a small plastic container. Fill it with soil and insert seeds in the soil. They should be covered with about ¼ " of soil. Water. Be patient...it takes a while for seeds to sprout.

2. **AVOCADO PIT**

   Stick 3 toothpicks into the side of the avocado pit, to hold it in the neck of the jar or glass so that the tip is in the water. Keep it in a warm place out of direct sunlight. Add water from time to time to keep the tip wet. When roots have formed (it may take 6 weeks) and the stem has appeared, plant in soil. Don't cover the top of the seed.

3. **GRASS SEED**

   Sprinkle some on a damp sponge. Keep it damp and presto.

4. **PINEAPPLE TOP**

   Slice off the top of a fresh pineapple and place the fruit part in a jar of water. The jar should support the foliage while the fruit part hangs in water. Roots and new leaves will grow. When roots have formed, plant in soil.

5. **CARROT TOP**

   Remove leaves from the carrot, if necessary. Slice ½ " off the top. Put this in a shallow dish of water and wait.

6. **CELERY HEART**

   Put the inside part of the celery bunch (heart and a few small leaves) in a small glass with water.

7. **SWEET POTATO**

   Place potato in a jar with toothpicks, as described for avocado. Either end of the potato will do. After the roots have formed and the stem has appeared, plant in soil. You may be surprised to discover what a lovely delicate plant this clumsy vegetable produces.

30

8. **LIMA BEAN**

Line a glass jar with a damp paper towel. Place the lima bean between the towel and the jar so you can see it from the outside. Cover the jar.

Note: These specially grown plants will make nice presents for special friends or family, or can be raised to donate to your school fair or bazaar.

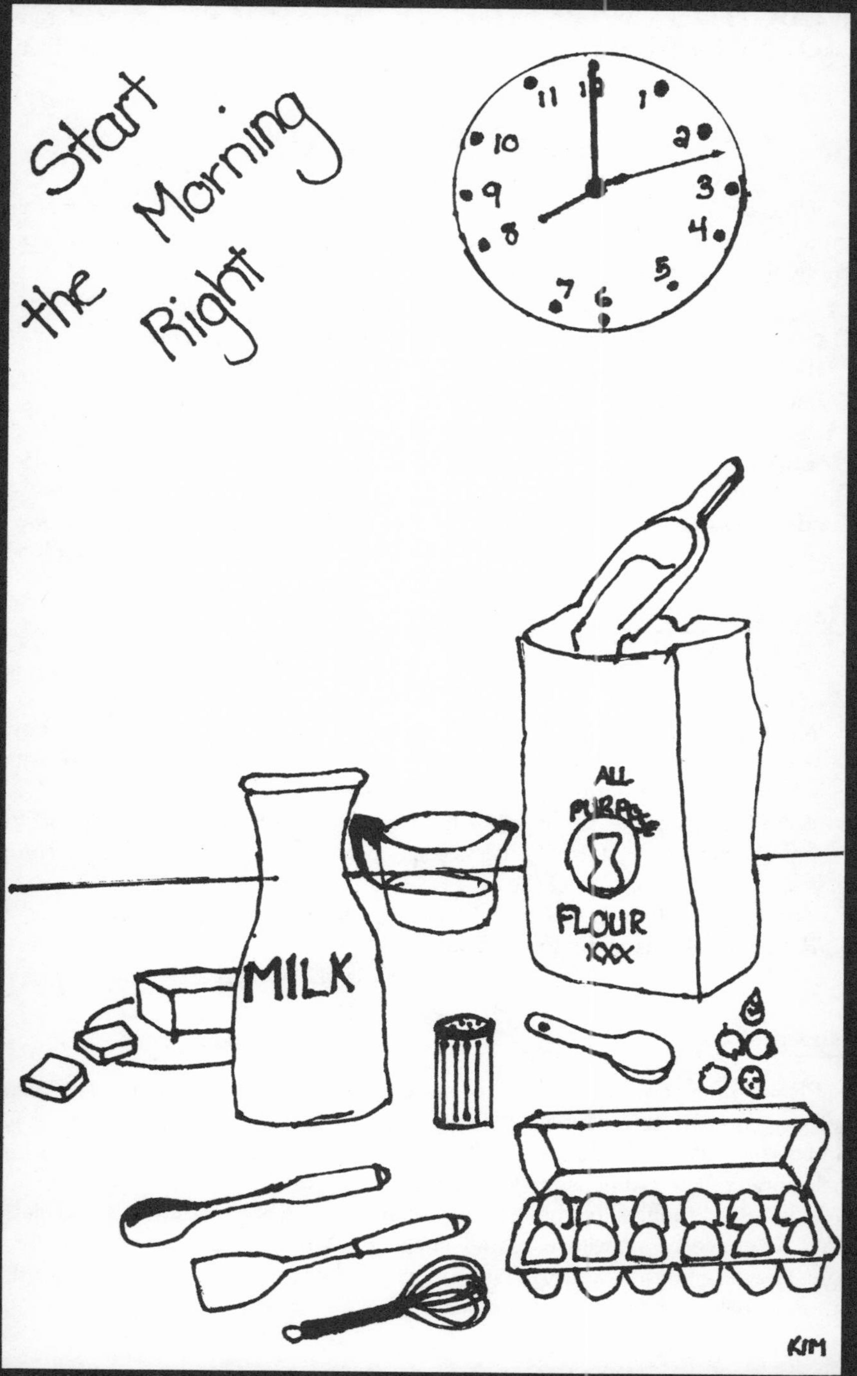
Start the Morning Right
ALL PURPOSE
FLOUR
XXX
MILK
KIM

BLUEBERRY MUFFINS

What could be nicer than warm muffins wrapped in a napkin on a morning breakfast table? They are quick and easy, particularly since the ingredients are only lightly mixed, not beaten smooth.

**2 cups all-purpose flour
    (hold aside ¼ cup of this)
3 teaspoons baking powder
½ teaspoon salt
½ cup sugar
1 egg, slightly beaten
1 cup milk**

**¼ cup melted butter
1 pint fresh blueberries
    (or 1 package frozen)**

**Cupcake pans
Shortening
Optional: paper cupcake liners
(this makes clean-up easier)**

How to Prepare:

1. Preheat the oven to 375.°
2. Grease the cupcake pans with the shortening or use paper liners.
3. Mix together the flour, baking powder, salt and sugar in a medium-sized bowl.
4. Add the egg, milk and butter, stirring only enough to dampen the flour. The batter should not be smooth.
5. Drain the blueberries and sprinkle them with ¼ cup reserved flour and mix this into the batter. (This should help the blueberries stay separated and not clump together at the bottom of the tin.)
6. Spoon the batter into the muffin tins only until they are two-thirds full.
7. Bake the muffins about 20 to 25 minutes.

Yield: 12 muffins

Note:

Properly mixed muffins should be stirred only until no flour shows. This batter will give you perfect muffins after baking, slightly rounded on the top, golden brown and glossy with a pebbled surface. The grain is uniform and no long holes or tunnels appear. The crumb is moist and tender.

Overmixed muffins that have been beaten until the batter is smooth and elastic have an uneven grain with large and small tunnels running up toward the pointed top. They are tough and dry. The top is peaked and misshapen, and the crust is smooth, pale and lacking in gloss.

**START THE
MORNING RIGHT**

Recipe Skill Level   Easy
Suggested Age Level   7 and Up

BRAN CEREAL MUFFINS

Vegetable shortening
  (to grease the muffin tins)
1 cup whole bran cereal
1 cup milk
1 egg
¼ cup vegetable oil

¼ cup honey
1¼ cups whole wheat flour,
  unsifted
2 teaspoons baking powder
¼ teaspoon baking soda
½ teaspoon salt

How to Prepare:

1. Preheat the oven to 400.°
2. Grease muffin tins with a little shortening or use paper cupcake liners.
3. Stir the bran cereal and the milk together. Let this mixture stand for a minute or two.
4. Now add the egg, oil and the honey and beat well. Set aside.
5. In a separate mixing bowl, mix together the dry ingredients which include the whole wheat flour, baking powder, baking soda and the salt.
6. Add the dry ingredients to the cereal mixture and stir only until it is blended. Do not over mix or the muffins will not rise properly and will have long tunnels in them.
7. With a tablespoon, fill each muffin tin two-thirds full.
8. Place muffins in the oven and bake about 20 to 25 minutes or until lightly browned.

Yield: 12 muffins

Culinary Note:

Bran and whole wheat flour are rich in natural fiber. Dietary fiber is plant material which is not digested in the gastrointestinal tract. Fiber is a plus in weight reduction because bulky foods will quickly fill you up.

Other sources of fiber are nuts, fruits, dried peas, dried beans and vegetables, particularly those that are unpeeled or have edible seeds.

Recipe Skill Level   Moderate
Suggested Age Level   7 and Up

ZUCCHINI WALNUT BREAD

Zucchini (Green Squash) belongs to the climbing family known as Cucurbitas, together with their cousins cucumbers, melons, decorative autumn gourds, pumpkins, spaghetti squash, acorn squash, butternut squash and Patty Pans to name just a few.

This recipe makes two 8"x4" loaves (baked in foil pans) or six 5"x3" loaves. It is wonderful for breakfast with butter or cream cheese and even tastes better the next day. It is good right out of the freezer in place of coffee cake. Take some along in your lunch box to school or for snacks after school.

2 cups sugar
1 cup vegetable oil
3 large eggs
1 Tablespoon ground cinnamon
1 teaspoon baking powder
1 teaspoon baking soda
1 teaspoon vanilla
½ teaspoon ground ginger
½ teaspoon salt

3¼ cups all-purpose flour
3 cups (shredded, unpeeled)
   zucchini, about 3 medium
1 cup walnuts, ground
1 cup shredded coconut

Waxed paper cut to fit the
   bottom of the foil tins
Shortening to grease the foil tins

How to Prepare:

1. Preheat the oven to 325.° Grease the pans generously with solid shortening and line the bottom of each pan with waxed paper and grease that.
2. Combine all ingredients, except flour, zucchini and walnuts, in a large bowl and beat for 2 minutes until blended.
3. Now fold in the flour until blended, then zucchini and walnuts.
4. Divide this mixture evenly between pans and bake them on the center rack in the oven until a wooden toothpick inserted in the center comes out clean. The center should feel firm to the touch. This will take about 1 hour and 15 minutes for the large loaves and 45 to 50 minutes for the small ones according to your oven (all oven temperatures vary). When done, remove them from the oven.
5. Cool the breads 5 minutes in the pans. Turn the breads out onto racks to cool completely. Remove the waxed paper. Using the waxed paper insures that the breads will not stick to the bottom of the pans.

NOTE: Frozen breads will keep for up to 3 months. Refrigerated breads will keep for a week and breads kept at room temperature, wrapped airtight, will keep for up to 3 days. These breads make lovely gifts but don't forget to include the recipe.

Recipe Skill Level   Easy
Suggested Age Level   10 and Up
(Oven assistance needed.)

CRUNCHY GRANOLA

Ingredients:

3 cups quick cooking oatmeal   **1 cup raisins**
1 cup unsweetened wheat germ   **½ cup oil**
½ cup coconut   **½ cup honey**
1 cup nuts (coarsely chopped)   **2 teaspoons vanilla**

How to Prepare:

1. Preheat the oven to 275.°
2. Mix oatmeal, wheat germ, coconut, nuts and raisins in a large bowl.
3. Mix oil, honey and vanilla. Pour over oat mixture. Stir lightly until evenly mixed.
4. Spread mixture on an ungreased 15″x10″x1″ baking pan.
5. Bake 1 hour, stirring each 15 minutes (use pot holders).
6. Cool. Break up in large lumps. Store in an airtight container.

Yield: Approx. 6½ cups

Recipe Skill Level   Easy
Suggested Age Level   6 and Up

CORN or APPLE FRITTERS

Corn or apples make this fritter a delightful addition to your breakfast table.

**½ cup canned corn
(fresh is best) or
½ cup chopped apples
1 egg, lightly beaten
3 Tablespoons all-purpose flour**

**¼ teaspoon baking powder
Pinch of salt
Pinch of freshly grated nutmeg
3 Tablespoons butter**

How to Prepare:

1. Combine corn (or apples) and egg in a medium-sized bowl.
2. Add the flour, baking powder, salt and nutmeg and mix well with a fork or whisk.
3. Melt the butter in a medium skillet over medium-high heat.
4. Drop batter into the skillet by tablespoon and fry fritter until browned on the bottom and bubbles appear.
5. Flip the fritter carefully over and continue to fry until the underside is brown.
6. Serve immediately.

Yield: Approx. 4 small

Culinary Note:

This is a great way to use leftover corn-on-the-cob.

START THE
MORNING RIGHT

Recipe Skill Level   Easy
Suggested Age Level   6 and Up
(Adult supervision necessary with
hot waffle iron.)

HANS BRINKER WAFFLES

Waffles are a traditional food in Holland. They are warm and toasty in cold weather, but they are also good in the summer with ice cream, cold honey or jam.

3 eggs
1¼ cups milk
¼ cup butter, melted
2 cups unbleached sifted flour

2 teaspoons baking powder
½ teaspoon salt
2 teaspoons sugar

Waffle iron

How to Prepare:

1. Preheat the waffle iron to medium heat.
2. Crack the eggs on the side of a large bowl and drop them into the bowl.
3. Add the milk to the eggs and blend together with a fork or a whisk.
4. Now add the melted butter and stir into the egg mixture.
5. In a small bowl, sift together the flour, baking powder, salt and sugar.
6. Add the dry ingredients slowly to the egg mixture. Set this aside.
7. In the meantime, melt a little shortening on the waffle iron (do not use butter because it burns very quickly). Check your waffle iron to see if it has an indicator light which indicates when it is ready to use.
8. Fill the lower section of the waffle iron about half full with the batter. Bring the cover down and cook until the waffle is lightly browned which should take about 5 minutes.
9. Loosen the edges of the waffle from the waffle iron with a fork and carefully remove it. Wait for the indicator light to go on again before you add the next waffle batter.

NOTE: Waffles freeze well. Just pop them out of your freezer into the toaster and they're ready to serve.

CAUTION: The waffle iron gets very hot and retains the heat for some time even when unplugged. Be very careful when you are cleaning up. Also note that the plug portion of the waffle iron should never be submerged in water.

Yield: Approx. 10 or 12

BLUEBERRY GRIDDLECAKES

¾ cup milk
  (at room temperature)
2 Tablespoons butter, melted
1 egg yolk and 1 egg white
1 cup all-purpose flour

2 teaspoons baking powder
2 Tablespoons sugar
½ teaspoon salt
½ cup blueberries
  (if frozen, strain before using)

How to Prepare:

1. In a medium-sized mixing bowl, beat milk, butter and egg yolk lightly.
2. Add flour, baking powder, sugar and salt. Stir only enough to dampen flour.
3. Add the blueberries and mix gently.
4. Beat egg white in an electric mixer until fluffy, then mix in gently with griddlecake batter.
5. Lightly grease a griddle pan or frying pan and set over a moderate heat until a drop of cold water sprinkled on the pan sizzles rapidly. Now you are ready to fry.
6. Pour approximately ¼ cup of the batter on the griddle and fry the cakes until little bubbles appear on the surface, then turn them over and fry for a minute more on the other side until done.
7. Serve immediately or keep some warm on a plate in 200° oven while the others are being done.
8. Serve with maple syrup, honey or pancake syrup.

NOTE: Leftover griddlecakes can be frozen. Simply layer them on sheets of waxed paper and wrap air-tight in plastic wrap. Lay these flat in the freezer until they are frozen, then you may rearrange their place in the freezer. To reheat, simply pop into a toaster oven or fry again briefly on a greased griddle or fry pan.
Yield: Approx. 6 to 8

Culinary Note:

To separate an egg, break it gently against a sturdy glass bowl. You will have one-half of the egg shell empty and the other half will have the egg yolk and white. Gently transfer the yolk from one half of the shell to the other, allowing the egg white to fall into the glass bowl. Do this carefully without breaking the yolk. It may take a little practice.

40

ITALIAN FRITTATA

A frittata is actually an Italian open-faced omelet. It can be made on the stove or in the oven. There is no limit to the number of fillings you can use. Try a variety of cheeses, vegetables, herbs or meats.

It is a great dish for company because both the company and the cook can sit down together to enjoy this treat. The chef does not have to stay in the kitchen and make everyone a different type egg.

BACON-CHEDDAR FRITTATA

**6 large eggs
2 Tablespoons butter
¼ cup onion, minced
1 cup milk
1 cup grated
   Cheddar cheese**

**1 cup bacon, cooked,
   cooled and diced
Dash of freshly grated
   pepper
¼ teaspoon salt**

How to Prepare:

1. Preheat the oven to 400.°
2. Beat the eggs in a medium-sized mixing bowl until the yolks and whites are well blended. Add salt and pepper.
3. Melt the butter in the skillet and sauté the onions.
4. Add the milk, onions, ¾ cup of cheese and the bacon to the egg mixture and stir well.
5. Butter a casserole or baking dish well and pour the mixture into the dish. Sprinkle with the remaining ¼ cup cheese.
6. Bake the frittata in the oven for 20 to 30 minutes or until it is set and golden brown.
7. Cut into slices and serve.

Yield: 4 servings

Lunch Box Ideas

LUNCH BOX IDEAS

TIPS FOR CHILDREN AND PARENTS

- Lunch fulfills one-third of the body's nutritional needs of the day. Be sure you pack the proper foods in that lunch box. Make sure food is fresh, good, and as free of undesirable ingredients as possible.

- Make lunchtime fun and enjoyable. Always include fresh vegetables. Dessert should be fresh fruit with a little sweet treat on occasion.

- Use cookie cutters to make sandwiches a surprise shape.

- If mornings are hurried, pack lunch the night before and keep refrigerated. Do not fill the thermos until the morning.

- Parents should monitor closely school lunch programs. If they are not nutritious and of poor quality, then let your concerns be known. Encourage other parents to voice their concerns. Children can also write letters to their student council or school newspaper.

- Vending machines can sabotage those nutritious lunches. Check your school machines. You can control what foods are in them by working with your principal or home and school association. Use the profit from a fresh fruit juice machine for a school play project.

- Organize a "Sugarless Wednesday" (or Thursday or Friday) at your school and have the school or neighborhood newspaper cover the event. Get the school nurse involved and monitor lunches in the lunchroom. Include a poster contest. How about a "Green and Gold Day" using all nutritious food of that color? It could be terrific.

- Include colorful napkins, plastic utensils, fancy straws or a special love note.

- Wide-mouthed thermoses are wonderful for soups or fresh fruit salad.

- If you freeze a sandwich, it will be just the right temperature by lunchtime. Just spread butter or margarine on the bread to prevent the bread from getting soggy. Egg whites, jam, raw veggies and fresh fruit do not freeze well. On hot days, do not pack sandwiches with mayonnaise or desserts with custards, because they will go bad.

- Some children react strangely to food containing preservatives, artificial dyes, excess sugar or artificial sweeteners. If a child shows symptoms or is hyperactive, check with your doctor. It may be corrected easily by a change in diet.

- Lunch boxes and thermoses should be thoroughly washed with soap and hot water each day. A baby bottle brush works well to clean out thermos bottles.

LUNCH BOX IDEAS

TAKE-ALONG LUNCHES

With a little planning the day before, children as young as 5 or 6 can take the responsibility for packing their own lunches. Mom or dad can advise on what items are in the refrigerator and what items should be picked up at the grocery store. They can shop for quality and price and have a wonderful time doing both.

Sandwich Ideas

Start with an interesting bread:
bagels
pita bread
raisin bread
whole wheat-honey bread
English muffins
date nut bread
pumpernickle or rye bread
sourdough bread
high-protein bread

Filling Ideas:

Swiss cheese and apple slices
sliced chicken and pineapple
cream cheese and dried fruit
guacamole and tomatoes
salads, salads, salads (tuna, egg, turkey, salmon)
    with cucumbers, olives, bacon, bean sprouts, raisins,
    dates, sunflower seeds or dried apricots to name just a few.

Thermos Ideas (Avoid glass-lined thermos)

leftover soups and stews
fruit salad
pasta
chili

LUNCH BOX IDEAS

TAKE-ALONG LUNCHES (continued)

Thermos Ideas:

yogurt
cottage cheese
pudding
fruit juice
dip for raw veggies or chips

Dessert Ideas:

non-frosted ice box cakes
muffins
granola bars
seasonal fresh fruit
assorted cheese cubes
carob-coated raisins
raisins
melon balls
dried fruit and nut mixture
brownies for 6 (to share with friends)

Greens and Veggies

carrot curls or sticks
raw broccoli or cauliflower
blanched green beans
cherry tomatoes
green, red or yellow peppers
zucchini sticks
celery, plain or stuffed with peanut butter
radishes

PACKING

- A holiday napkin or fancy paper plates make lunch special.
- Use plastic sandwich containers to prevent sandwiches from getting squashed.
- Squashables, such as cherries or strawberries, should be packed in plastic containers.
- Remember that sour cream, mayonnaise and jam will make bread soggy, while margarine, butter and cream cheese will not.
- Many sandwiches freeze well, but leave out the lettuce and tomato. Pack them separately and arrange in your sandwich just before eating.

FOOD SAFETY

ALWAYS WASH YOUR HANDS WITH HOT WATER AND SOAP BEFORE HANDLING FOOD. WASH INSULATED CONTAINERS AND LUNCH BOXES DAILY IN HOT SUDSY WATER. RINSE AND DRY WELL WITH A CLEAN DISH TOWEL.

LUNCH BOX IDEAS

COLD PEACH SOUP

**5 large, ripe peaches, peeled
and quartered**
¼ cup sugar
1 cup sour cream
¼ cup fresh lemon juice

**3 Tablespoons orange juice
concentrate (thawed)**

**Garnish: sliced and peeled
fresh peaches
fresh mint leaves**

How to Prepare:

1. Puree 5 peaches with sugar in a blender or a food processor.
2. Mix in the sour cream.
3. Add the lemon juice and orange juice concentrate and blend until smooth.
4. Transfer to a bowl, cover and refrigerate until well chilled.
5. Ladle soup into bowls.
6. Garnish with sliced fresh peaches and mint. Serve.

Yield: Approx. 4 to 6 servings

Culinary Note:

Peaches are a fragile fruit and should be handled gently. They should feel firm with a little give. Greenish fruit should be avoided as it will never ripen at home. Store ripe peaches in the refrigerator, but those that are a little too firm are best kept at room temperature.

Yogurt can be substituted for the sour cream if you would like.

LUNCH BOX IDEAS

HOAGIE

If you plan to use this for lunch, you will have to start the day before to make the bread and finish it off in the morning with the fillings before you leave for school.

French Bread Recipe

1½ teaspoons dry active yeast
¾ cup warm water
1 teaspoon sugar
¾ teaspoon salt

1 Tablespoon butter or margarine
2 to 2¼ cups all-purpose flour
** (or bread flour)**
1 teaspoon cornmeal

How to Prepare Hoagie Roll:

1. Preheat the oven to 375°.
2. In a large mixing bowl, dissolve the yeast in warm water and add the sugar. Stir the mixture to dissolve the yeast and let the mixture rest for 5 minutes. It should begin to foam and bubble which means the yeast is alive and fresh.
3. Now add the salt, butter and 1 cup of the flour.
4. Beat this with a wooden spoon until it is thoroughly mixed.
5. Gradually add the remaining 1 cup of flour until the dough is easy to handle.
6. Place onto a well floured surface and knead for 5 to 10 minutes or until the dough is elastic and not sticky.
7. Place the dough in a greased bowl, cover and let it rise in a warm place for about 1 hour or until it is double in size, which may take an hour depending on the heat of the kitchen.
8. Punch down the dough and shape into a long loaf. Place the loaf on a baking pan which has been sprinkled with cornmeal.
9. Leave the dough to rest and rise for a second time for about 35 to 40 minutes until it has again doubled in size.
10. Bake the loaf in a preheated oven for 20 to 25 minutes or until golden brown.
11. Remove the pan at once. After it has cooled for 5 or 10 minutes, slice the bread in half lengthwise.

How to Make a Hoagie:

Let your imagination carry you away. Invent a new one. Use leftovers.

Suggested fillings: ham, capacola, salami, cheese, shredded lettuce, sliced tomatoes, sliced onions, hot peppers, oregano, a little olive oil, etc., etc., etc.

Wrap your hoagie well if you plan to take it to school for lunch. It leaks oil and can make a mess of clothes or school books in your lunch bag.

Yield: 4 large or 2 small

49

LUNCH BOX IDEAS

TOMATO STUFFED WITH FRESH SALMON SALAD

4 fresh tomatoes
1 pound fresh salmon
cooked and cooled
(canned, if unavailable)
¼ cup onion, chopped
1 stalk celery,
peeled and chopped

1 teaspoon fresh dill, chopped
4 sprigs fresh dill (for garnish)

Dressing: 1 cup mayonnaise
(approximately)
Salt and pepper to
taste
Lettuce leaves,
rinsed and drained
on paper towels

How to Prepare:

1. Rinse the tomatoes under cold running water and drain on paper towels.
2. With a paring knife, carefully remove the core and slice off about ¼ " off the top of each tomato.
3. Scoop out the center of the tomatoes with a spoon and discard the center pieces (or you can save these in the freezer for a good tomato sauce). Be very gentle when you are handling the tomatoes so you do not change the shape by squeezing them too hard.
4. Gently flake the salmon with a fork, discarding any stray bones you may find.
5. In a medium-sized bowl, combine the salmon, onion, celery, chopped dill and the dressing.
6. Taste the salad and add salt and pepper if you like.
7. Fill the tomatoes with the salmon salad and garnish each with a sprig of fresh dill.
8. Place the tomatoes on a bed of lettuce and enjoy. If you plan to transport them to school or a picnic, cushion the tomatoes with lettuce in a plastic container so they do not roll. Also remember that fish and mayonnaise are very perishable, so try to eat both fairly quickly. If they sit out unrefrigerated all day, then simply throw them out rather than risk getting sick.

NOTE: You can also use tuna salad, chicken salad or any of your favorites.
Yield: 4 servings

50

Culinary Note:

The salmon is known as the king of fish. Spawned in fresh water, it spends most of its life in the sea, only returning to fresh water, usually to the river where it was born, to spawn. In fresh water, salmon takes no food, so on their way back to the sea, they are miserably thin and spent and certainly not fit to eat. Spring and summer are the best times to buy fresh salmon. They are sold whole or in steaks. When they are really fresh, there is a creamy substance between the flakes of flesh which sets to a curd when cooked. Avoid steaks that look soft, greyish, oily or watery.

Recipe Skill Level   Easy
Suggested Age Level 3 and Up

TRAIL MIX or "GORP"

This is an all-purpose energy snack that can be used for hiking or long car rides. Transport gorp in plastic sandwich bags secured with a twisty tie.

2 cups raisins
½ cup unsalted peanuts
  or walnuts
½ cup dried fruit (apple,
  apricots or bananas)

½ cup coconut
¼ cup wheat germ
¼ cup sunflower seeds
  (optional)

How to Prepare:

1. Toss all the ingredients together in a large bowl.
2. Store in an airtight jar.

NOTE: You can also add a little of your favorite non-sugary dry cereal to this recipe.
Yield: Approx. 4 cups

AFTER SCHOOL IDEAS

Recipe Skill Level   Easy
Suggested Age Level   5 and Up
(Assistance needed with knife.)

KWANZAA BANANA BOATS

8 large ripe bananas
2 cups fresh pineapple, chopped
1 cup heavy whipping cream
¼ cup confectioners sugar

1 teaspoon vanilla
2 Tablespoons brown sugar
1 cup nuts, chopped

How to Prepare:

1. Wipe off the banana skins with a damp paper towel.
2. With a small knife, cut a 1" strip along the length of the inside curve of the bananas. Remove the strip carefully and discard.
3. Scoop out the pulp with a spoon. Mash the pulp and add the pineapple.
4. Put the banana skins on a shallow plate and fill them with the fruit.
5. Whip the heavy cream in an electric mixer at high speed, slowly adding confectioners sugar, brown sugar and the vanilla.
6. Top banana boats with the sweetened whipped cream and sprinkle them with nuts and chill. Serve cold.

Yield: 8 servings

NOTE: Kwanzaa is an African-American celebration. It is not a religious holiday or an alternative to Christmas. Kwanzaa is a special time when black families and friends come together to give thanks and to celebrate their African heritage. The word Kwanzaa in Swahili means "first fruit" and originated in 1967 as a harvest celebration.

Recipe Skill Level   Easy
Suggested Age Level 3 and Up

FRESH FRUIT POPS

Inexpensive plastic popsicle molds are available in most large supermarkets in the non-food section. Paper cups with wooden popsicle sticks may also be used.

Fill them with pure unsweetened juice such as apple, orange, pineapple, apricot or pear nectar and store them in your freezer until hardened.

If you have a food processor or blender available, puree fresh fruit such as strawberries, pears, kiwi, etc. and freeze this in your popsicle molds.

They are a great treat anytime for child or adult alike and won't spoil dinner.

AFTER SCHOOL IDEAS

Recipe Skill Level   Easy
Suggested Age Level 3 and Up

FRUIT KABOBS

6 fresh strawberries
1 large apple, peeled, cored and
  sliced into 6 slices
½ pound seedless green grapes

1 slice fresh pineapple
  (6 chunks)
1 banana, sliced

Toothpicks

How to Prepare:

1. Gently wash the fruit and drain on paper towels.
2. Alternate fruit evenly onto 6 toothpicks.
3. Serve.

NOTE: This is a great snack for visitors that you can make quickly by yourself. You may also pack this for lunch, but sprinkle the apple and banana with a little lemon juice to keep it from turning brown.

Yield: 6 servings

AFTER SCHOOL IDEAS

PEANUT BUTTER BALLS

These are not only delicious but very high in protein. Best blended in a food processor, they can be mixed with a little muscle-power and a wooden spoon.

2 cups peanut butter   **⅔ cup honey**
1 cup non-fat dry powdered milk

                                            Optional: 1 cup graham cracker
                                                     crumbs, crushed or
                                            1 cup wheat germ

How to Prepare:

1. Combine peanut butter, powdered milk and honey together in a bowl with a wooden spoon or in a food processor.
2. Shape the mixture into balls and roll gently in graham cracker crumbs or wheat germ.
3. Freeze until ready to eat. These never become too hard because of the high oil content.

Yield: 24

BEST EVER PIZZA

The word "pizza" means PIE in Italian. Mozzarella, the skim milk variety, gives pizza its characteristic long strands.

Basic Pizza Dough

1 package dry yeast
1 teaspoon light brown sugar
¾ cup warm water
2¼ cups all-purpose flour
½ teaspoon salt
2 Tablespoons olive oil

Garnish: 1 cup mozzarella
cheese, grated
½ cup Italian tomato
sauce or marinara
sauce
½ cup mushrooms,
pepperoni or sausages,
or all of these

How to Prepare:

1. Preheat the oven to 400.°
2. Dissolve yeast with the sugar in ½ cup warm water. Set aside for 5 minutes while yeast dissolves and begins to bubble and foam.
3. Sift 2 cups flour together with salt into a large mixing bowl. Make a well in the middle of the flour and add 1 Tablespoon of oil and ¼ cup warm water.
4. Add dissolved yeast mixture and mix well.
5. Turn dough onto a floured board and knead for 8 to 10 minutes or until smooth and elastic, adding flour, as necessary, to keep the dough from being too sticky.
6. Place dough in a clean bowl which has been brushed with oil. Brush dough with oil and cover. Let dough rise in a warm place for 1½ hours.
7. Remove dough from bowl and place on a floured board. With a rolling pin, roll out dough to fit one 12″ pizza pan.
8. Spoon sauce over pizza and sprinkle mozzarella cheese over sauce.
9. Add whatever extra topping that you wish.
10. Bake pizza until the crust browns, about 15 to 20 minutes. Enjoy.

Yield: 1 large

Culinary Note:

Invent a new pizza, try:

A Goldilocks Pizza — lox and onions

A Popeye Pizza — spinach, olive oil and sweet peas

A Four Cheese Pizza — ricotta, provolone, Parmesan, mozzarella, mixed with heavy cream

A Mexican Pizza — ground beef, taco sauce, monterey jack cheese, Cheddar cheese and a 6-ounce can of drained jalapeno peppers.

AFTER SCHOOL IDEAS

Recipe Skill Level   Easy
Suggested Age Level   12 and Up
(This recipe requires working with a very hot pot over the stove, and older children may be able to work more independently.)

POPCORN

Popcorn is a low-calorie snack which is filling and also fun to make.

3 Tablespoons of vegetable oil   **Salt (optional)**
½ cup popcorn kernels
3 to 4 Tablespoons melted butter   **4 quart heavy pot and lid**
(optional)

How to Prepare:

1. Put oil in a 4 quart heavy pot with a lid and let it heat over a medium heat for 30 seconds.
2. Slip in 3 corn kernels into the pot. When they pop, the pot is hot enough.
3. Stir in the remainder of the corn kernels and shake the pot gently so they are evenly covered with the oil. Keep one hand on the lid and one hand on the handle.
4. Continue to move the pot gently and continuously back and forth until the popping stops.
5. Carefully remove the pot from the stove and turn the popcorn into a large bowl. Toss out any unpopped kernels (these are very bad for your teeth).
6. Plain popcorn is wonderful, but for an occasional treat, add the melted butter and a sprinkling of salt.

Yield: Approx. 8 to 10 cups

59

Recipe Skill Level   Easy
                                    Suggested Age Level   5 and Up

CRANBERRY PUNCH

2 quarts cranberry juice cocktail   **2 quarts ginger ale**
2 small cans fresh lemonade,   **Pitted cherries**
** thawed**

                                             Punch bowl
                                             Ice

How to Prepare:

1. Pour the cranberry juice cocktail, the lemonade and the ginger ale over ice in
   a punch bowl.
2. Mix slightly to blend the flavors and to combine the lemonade.
3. Garnish the punch with cherries if desired and serve.

Yield: 25 to 30

*NOTE: Although a 5-year-old can prepare this recipe, it can also be enjoyed by a
baby brother or baby sister. Ask mom or dad first, but cranberry juice has been known
to help diaper rash. It seems to neutralize the acidity.*

Dinner's Ready

DINNER'S READY

"SALAD BAR NIGHT"

Clear the dining room table and set up for your own "Salad Bar".

Do all your preparation work in the kitchen to keep any mess in one place and so you will be close to the sink for rinsing vegetables.

There is no limit to your choices. Here are just a few suggestions:

Romaine or red-tipped lettuce
Watercress
Fresh parsley, chopped
Cherry or plum tomatoes, sliced
Fresh spinach, cleaned
Carrots
Green or red or yellow peppers
Avocado, sliced
Snow peas
Zucchini
Mushrooms
Celery
Sprouts
Red salad onions or scallions
Cheese
Fresh herbs
Water chestnuts
Broccoli, blanched
Nuts
Pasta, cooked and cooled
Radishes
Cucumbers

Salad Dressings

It is a good idea to check with mom or dad for some organizational planning. You may wish to use paper plates tonight to make it an easy night for the chef after dinner. Complete your dinner with a loaf of good dark bread and some iced tea or lemonade.

DINNER'S READY

Recipe Skill Level   Easy
Suggested Age Level   5 and up

SALAD NICOISE

This is a Mediterranean salad from Nice, a city on the Riviera.

1 head red or green-tipped
  lettuce
1 small can tuna, drained and
  flaked
1 pound fresh green beans,
  blanched
1 cup ziti, cooked and cooled
½ cup pitted black olives
3 hard boiled eggs, shelled
  and rinsed

4 tomatoes, sliced in quarters
1 small can anchovies, drained
  and chopped (optional)
6 Tablespoons olive oil
1 Tablespoon wine vinegar
1 clove garlic, minced
Salt and pepper to taste
½ cup fresh parsley, chopped

How to Prepare:

1. Separate the lettuce leaves and rinse them gently in a colander under cold running water. Drain them on paper towels.
2. In a large salad bowl, arrange the lettuce, tuna, green beans, ziti, black olives, hard boiled eggs and tomatoes.
3. In a small mixing bowl, mix together the anchovies, olive oil, wine vinegar, garlic, salt, pepper and fresh parsley. Mix the dressing well with a wire whisk or a fork.
4. Pour the dressing over the salad and toss gently.
5. Serve immediately.

Yield: 6 servings

Culinary Note:

To blanch means to plunge vegetables (or fruits) in boiling water for a short period of time to precook. This quick method also helps maintain the color and flavor.

To mince means to cut or chop into very fine pieces.

SPINACH SALAD

1 pound fresh spinach leaves
6 thick slices bacon, cooked
  and minced
½ cup fresh mushrooms, sliced
Salt and pepper to taste
½ teaspoon basil

¼ teaspoon garlic powder
1 hard boiled egg

¼ cup fresh lemon juice
2 Tablespoons vinegar
½ teaspoon sugar

How to Prepare:

1. Gently wash spinach and lay to dry on paper towels. Discard stems and any bruised leaves.
2. Pull apart and place in a salad bowl.
3. Cook bacon on frying pan, drain, cool and cut into small pieces. Add bacon to the salad.
4. Slice mushrooms and place in the salad bowl.
5. Slice the hard boiled egg and add to your salad with the seasonings.
6. Combine the fresh lemon juice, vinegar and sugar, stirring well with a fork or a whisk and add to your salad.
7. Toss the spinach salad with the dressing and serve very cold. This salad should be served immediately once it has been dressed. This salad can always be prepared ahead of time, and then at the last minute, add the dressing so the spinach does not wilt and get soggy.

Yield: 6 servings

Recipe Skill Level   Moderate
Suggested Age Level   9 and Up

BROCCOLI QUICHE

*1 pie crust, unbaked
2 cups heavy cream
4 large eggs
¾ teaspoon salt
Dash of pepper, cayenne and
   nutmeg

4 ounces Jarlsberg cheese,
   grated
1½ cups broccoli, cooked
   and chopped
2 Tablespoons Parmesan cheese,
   finely grated

How to Prepare:

1. Preheat the oven to 375° for 10 minutes.
2. Bake the pie crust for 15 minutes or until it is lightly browned. Cool completely.
3. With a fork or a whisk, blend together the heavy cream, eggs, salt, pepper, cayenne and nutmeg. Set this aside.
4. Sprinkle the pie shell with the cheese, then the broccoli, and pour the cream mixture over all.
5. With a finger, stir the broccoli mixture gently to even out the color.
6. Sprinkle the top with the Parmesan cheese.
7. Turn the oven temperature down to 325.°
8. Without spilling, carefully transfer the quiche to the oven and bake at 325° for 45 minutes or until the middle is set.
9. Cool the quiche for 15 minutes before slicing. The custard should have an opportunity to set for a few minutes.

Yield: 6 servings

*Basic Pie Crust recipe can be found in the BAKING AND DESSERT MAKING section.

Culinary Note:

Cheddar or Gruyere cheese may be substituted for the Jarlsberg if you like.

Recipe Skill Level   Moderate
Suggested Age Level 9 and Up

FRESH ASPARAGUS QUICHE

This custard is rich and tender. Quiche is excellent for dinner or picnics and does not have to be served hot.

*1 pie crust, unbaked
¼ cup sour cream
3 egg yolks
2 whole eggs
1 cup light or heavy cream
⅓ cup milk
1 teaspoon salt
Freshly ground black pepper
¼ teaspoon grated nutmeg

3 Tablespoons butter
1 Tablespoon shallots, minced
½ lb. fresh asparagus
   (approximately 1½ cups)
   slightly undercooked and
   1″ in length
⅔ cup Swiss cheese, grated
Cayenne pepper, dash

How to Prepare:

1. Prepare the pie crust as noted in this cookbook. Set aside.
2. Preheat the oven to 425.°
3. Roll out the pastry and fit it into a 9″ pie plate.
4. To prepare the filling, mix together the sour cream, egg yolks, eggs, cream, milk, salt, pepper and nutmeg. Taste and correct the seasonings and reserve.
5. Melt 1½ Tablespoons of butter in a skillet and toss the shallots until they are soft.
6. Add the asparagus and toss for a minute or two over high heat. Remove from the heat and reserve.
7. Sprinkle one-half of the cheese into the shell and spread the asparagus mixture over this. Then add the remaining cheese to the shell.
8. Now pour the custard carefully over the asparagus, being careful not to overfill.
9. Dot with butter that is remaining and add a dash of cayenne pepper.
10. Put the quiche in the oven and bake at 425° for 10 minutes, then lower the temperature to 350° and bake for another 25 to 30 minutes or until the top is golden brown and slightly puffed.
11. Serve immediately or at room temperature.

Yield: 6 servings

*Basic Pie Crust recipe can be found in the BAKING AND DESSERT MAKING section.

Culinary Note:

To correct seasonings means to taste what you are making and add more seasonings if you feel it is necessary to make the recipe better.

Recipe Skill Level   Moderate
Suggested Age Level   12 and Up

POTATOES WITH THREE PEPPERS

6 to 8 potatoes
3 Tablespoons vegetable or
    corn oil
1/3 cup scallions, sliced
1/2 teaspoon salt (or to taste)
Freshly ground pepper

1/3 cup sweet green pepper
    (cubed)
1/3 cup sweet yellow pepper
    (cubed)
1/3 cup sweet red pepper (cubed)
1 Tablespoon butter

How to Prepare:

1. Peel the potatoes and cut them into 1/2" cubes. Drop the potatoes into a pot of cold water in between peeling and cutting so they do not turn brown.
2. Fill a small saucepan, large enough to hold the potatoes, with cold water and bring to a boil.
3. Add the potatoes and simmer for 1 to 2 minutes. Drain well.
4. Heat the oil in a skillet and add the drained potatoes. Cook, stirring and shaking the skillet as necessary, until the potatoes become golden, about 8 to 10 minutes.
5. Now add the scallions, salt, pepper and the three varieties of peppers and cook them, stirring gently, about 3 minutes.
6. Add the butter and cook another 2 minutes. The contrast in colors is beautiful.
7. Serve immediately.

NOTE: If yellow peppers are not available in your area, you may change the recipe to 1/2 cup green and 1/2 cup red peppers.

DINNER'S READY

Recipe Skill Level   Moderate
Suggested Age Level   12 and Up
(Adult supervision necessary in working with hot oil.)

HANUKAH HOLIDAY TREAT

Potato-Cheese Latkes

(Potato Pancakes)

A presentation of one's own special food is an expression of one's personality and background. Fried foods and Eastern European potato latkes are dishes symbolic of the miracle of the one-day supply of oil which burned for 8 days on the first Hanukah more than 2,100 years ago.

**1 medium baking potato
(all moisture removed)
2 cloves garlic, chopped
¾ cup scallions, chopped
½ cup Swiss cheese, grated
1 egg, lightly beaten**

**1 cup all-purpose flour
1 Tablespoon sugar
½ teaspoon salt
½ teaspoon pepper
Cooking oil**

How to Prepare:

1. Peel the potato and grate with a grater or process in the food processor.
2. Wrap the potato in a clean kitchen tea towel and squeeze to remove as much of the moisture as possible.
3. In a large bowl, mix together the potato with the garlic, scallion, cheese and the egg. Blend well.
4. In another bowl, sift together the flour, sugar, salt and pepper.
5. Blend the flour mixture into the potato mixture and form into little patties.
6. Fry the latkes in ¼″ hot cooking oil until golden brown, about 1½ minutes on each side. IMPORTANT: Have an adult on hand when frying with hot oil.
7. Serve the latkes hot. They are wonderful with sour cream and applesauce, or yogurt mixed with chives.

NOTE: Leftovers can be stored in the refrigerator and enjoyed the next day by simply popping them into a toaster oven for a few minutes.

Yield: 6 servings

DINNER'S READY

Recipe Skill Level   Easy
Suggested Age Level   6 and Up
(Adult help needed with peeling and
slicing apples.)

CIDER APPLESAUCE

This recipe is good with any all-purpose apples which are good for eating, salads and for most cooking, such as Baldwin, Jonathan, Stayman, Winesap and McIntosh.

2 pounds tart apples
⅔ cup cider (unpasteurized)
2 Tablespoons fresh lemon juice

2 teaspoons lemon rind, grated
⅓ cup sugar
⅛ teaspoon salt

How to Prepare:

1. Peel, core and cut apples into ¼ " thick wedges.
2. In a saucepan, combine apples with cider, lemon juice and lemon rind and bring to a boil over moderately high heat.
3. Reduce the heat and simmer the mixture for 15 minutes or until apples are almost tender.
4. Now add the sugar and salt and break the apples into pieces with a fork.
5. Cook the mixture for 5 minutes more and let the mixture cool.

Yield: Approx. 6 to 8 servings

Culinary Note:

Cidermaking is an autumn tradition. This tradition has remained unchanged for centuries. The apples go into a chopper and the resulting mash is wrapped in cloth sacking and stacked on wooden racks. The cider press pushes down on the racks, squeezing and filtering the juice through the cloth. The juices run down into a collection vat and from this vat, kegs and jugs are filled. The result of this cider process is a sweet, fresh, golden-brown cider that can be drunk on the spot.

Serving Suggestion: This dish can be enjoyed when it's warm with a pork entree.

DINNER'S READY

Recipe Skill Level   Easy
Suggested Age Level 5 and Up
(With supervision.)

HONEY BARBECUED CHICKEN

3 pounds chicken legs and thighs
1 egg yolk (save the egg white
   for another use)
1 teaspoon salt
⅛ teaspoon pepper
1 teaspoon paprika

2 Tablespoons soy sauce
1 Tablespoon fresh lemon juice
2 Tablespoons butter, melted
¼ cup honey

Roasting pan

How to Prepare:

1. Preheat the oven to 400.°
2. Rinse the chicken pieces well under cold running water and drain on paper towels.
3. In a large bowl, combine the yolk, salt, pepper, paprika, soy sauce, lemon juice, butter and honey.
4. Dip the chicken pieces into this mixture and arrange in the roasting pan.
5. Pour the rest of the sauce over the chicken.
6. Bake the chicken for 30 to 40 minutes.
7. Turn the chicken pieces over, carefully using a pair of tongs, and bake for an additional 30 minutes or until tender.

NOTE: This also works beautifully on the outdoor grill, but instead of pouring the excess sauce over the chicken, use a pastry brush and baste the chicken while it cooks. This will keep it moist and add flavor.

Yield: 6 to 8 servings

Culinary Note:

See page 40 for instructions on separating an egg.

DINNER'S READY

Recipe Skill Level   Easy
Suggested Age Level   8 and Up
(Adult supervision may be necessary
for oven use and testing for
doneness.)

ROCK CORNISH GAME HENS

This is a lovely cooking project when there are special dinner guests like Grand-mom and Grandpop. Serve one hen to a person, garnished with watercress.

4 Rock Cornish game hens
4 Tablespoons butter
½ teaspoon thyme, crumbled
½ teaspoon marjoram
salt

freshly ground pepper
1 cup chicken broth

Garnish: 1 bunch watercress
(washed gently and
drained)

How to Prepare:

1. Preheat oven to 400.°
2. Rub the hens all over with butter and sprinkle with crumbled thyme, marjoram, salt and pepper.
3. Place the hens, not touching, in a shallow pan and roast, basting every 10 to 15 minutes with chicken broth.
4. After 15 minutes have passed, reduce the heat to 300° and roast another 30 to 40 minutes, or until the juices run clear when a small slit is made in the upper thigh.
5. Serve with pan juices as a natural sauce. Garnish hens with watercress.

Serving Suggestion: Brown rice and fresh green beans would go nicely with this dish. Boxed stuffing mixes are also available which make stuffing-making very easy for children.

Yield: 4 servings

Culinary Note:

Dried herbs must be crumbled in your hand before they are added to a dish. This breaks them up and releases the oil and flavor.

DINNER'S READY

Recipe Skill Level   Moderate
Suggested Age Level   10 and Up
(IMPORTANT: Have an adult on
hand when frying with hot oil.)

SWEET AND SOUR CHICKEN

This is great picnic food. Put down a patchwork quilt, white paper napkins, a cold drink cooler and let the food be the star of the show.

12 chicken legs and thighs
¼ teaspoon salt
2 eggs, beaten
½ cup cornstarch
½ cup cooking oil

¾ cup sugar
1 cup pineapple juice
½ cup ketchup
½ cup chicken broth
2 Tablespoons soy sauce

How to Prepare:

1. Preheat the oven to 350.°
2. Season the chicken with salt.
3. Now coat the chicken with the egg and cornstarch.
4. In a large skillet, heat the cooking oil until it is very hot.
5. Carefully brown the chicken and remove to a waiting baking dish.
6. Combine the sugar, pineapple juice, ketchup, chicken broth and soy sauce in a medium saucepan. Bring the mixture to a boil, then pour over the chicken in the baking dish.
7. Place baking dish in the oven and bake for 45 minutes or until the chicken is tender and golden brown.
8. Cool and refrigerate until ready to pack for picnics or school lunches. It is also wonderful hot right from the oven for dinner.

Yield: 6 servings

HAMBURGERS WITH PEPPERCORN SAUCE

1½ pounds ground sirloin
1½ to 2 Tablespoons crushed
  peppercorns
2 Tablespoons butter
1 Tablespoon shallots
  (finely chopped)

¼ cup beef stock
  (fresh or canned)
3 Tablespoons fresh parsley
  (finely chopped)
Salt

How to Prepare:

1. Preheat the broiler to 350.°
2. Shape the meat into 6 equal patties. Sprinkle with salt and crushed peppercorns. Press down on the meat to help the peppercorns stick.
3. Broil the burgers 3 to 4 minutes in an ovenproof pan on each side, depending on thickness. Watch broiling carefully, so the meat is not overcooked.
4. Remove the patties to a warm platter.
5. In a skillet, add 1 Tablespoon butter and the shallots and cook until the shallots are wilted.
6. Add the beef stock and cook until reduced to about 2 Tablespoons.
7. Swirl in the remaining butter and add patties turning once off the heat.
8. Garnish with the fresh chopped parsley.

Yield: 6 servings

Culinary Note:

There are two kinds of PEPPER, black pepper from the East and red pepper from America. The term "white pepper" is dried seeds from the black pepper, which is milder than black pepper or peppercorns, as black pepper is called before it is ground.

SHALLOTS are a member of the onion family. They have a subtle flavor which is a cross between an onion and garlic.

DINNER'S READY

Recipe Skill Level   Difficult
Suggested Age Level   11 and Up
(Adult-child project.)

TORTELLINI FILLED WITH PARSLEY AND RICOTTA

NOTE: It is necessary to have a pasta machine for this recipe. A crank-type pasta machine is just fine.

Tortellini begin as circles. When they are stuffed and folded over, the edges do not come exactly together. Bend them around your finger and press one corner over the other. This is an adult-child project but lots of fun, especially for an artistic child.

Filling

⅓ cup fresh parsley   **Salt**
   (finely chopped)   **1 egg yolk**
1¼ cup fresh ricotta   **¼ teaspoon nutmeg**
1 cup Parmesan cheese (grated)

Cream Sauce

⅔ cup heavy cream   **3 Tablespoons butter**

Homemade Pasta Dough:

3 eggs   **1 Tablespoon milk or water**
2¼ cups all-purpose flour   **⅛ teaspoon salt**

How to Prepare Homemade Pasta Dough by Hand:

1. Measure flour into a bowl with the salt. Make a well in the center and add the eggs and the water or milk.
2. With wooden spoon, combine mixture until pastry comes together into a ball. You may have to add a little more flour as you work, but just flour your hands and keep working. (Adding flour directly to the dough may add too much flour and make the dough dry.)
3. Combine and form into three balls. Wrap two, so they don't dry out, and work with the remaining one.

<u>TORTELLINI</u> (continued)

<u>How to Prepare the Filling:</u>

1. Combine the parsley, ricotta, Parmesan, ½ teaspoon salt, egg yolk and nutmeg in a mixing bowl and mix well with a fork. Taste the mixture and correct the seasonings, then set aside.

NOW YOU ARE READY TO START
PUTTING THE TORTELLINI TOGETHER.

1. Have an adult help you put together the hand-cranked pasta machine and to start to roll out the dough, one ball at a time. The pasta machine takes a little practice but even a young child can do it, and it is great fun. Make sure the pasta machine is securely screwed down to your work table so it does not slip around. (Roll pasta according to manufacturer's directions.)
2. Using one sheet of pasta at a time, cut out 2½" circles with a cookie cutter or glass and put in ¼ teaspoon of filling in the center of each circle. Fold the circle over after you moisten the edges of the circle with a little water on your fingertip to seal the dough. Bend the half circle around your finger and press one corner over the other. Set aside.
3. Boil 3 quarts of water until it reaches a rapid boil. Carefully drop the tortellini into the boiling water and wait until it returns to a rapid boil. Stirring occasionally, cook the pasta until tender, about 8 to 10 minutes. The tortellini will rise to the top of the pot when they are tender. Carefully remove one tortellini, let it cool for a moment, and taste to see if it is done. Drain in a colander.
4. For the sauce, melt the butter and slowly add the heavy cream.
5. Serve warm and toss with the tortellini.

Yield: 6 to 8 servings

<u>Culinary Note:</u>

The parsley-ricotta filling will not keep, so plan to cook the tortellini the same day as you make them. The best way to freeze tortellini is to place them on a cookie sheet, uncooked, and place them in the freezer. When they are hard, remove the cookie sheet and place the tortellini in plastic bags tied securely so they remain air-tight. Return them to the freezer.

Recipe Skill Level   Medium
Suggested Age Level   10 and Up

BROWN RICE

Brown rice is a healthy addition to your meal. Use this as a side dish or a main dish adding leftovers.

½ cup scallions (chopped)
1 Tablespoon butter
1 bouillon cube (crushed)
2 cups beef stock
(fresh or canned)

1 cup long grain brown rice
Salt and pepper to taste
Optional: ½ cup leftover roast
beef or chicken (in pieces)

How to Prepare:

1. Saute scallions in butter and add the crushed bouillon cube in a medium saucepan.
2. Add the stock and bring to a boil.
3. Add the rice, salt and pepper, stir once and cover.
4. Turn temperature to low and simmer for 45 minutes.
5. After 45 minutes, turn off the heat and let the rice sit for 10 minutes without lifting the lid.
6. Remove cover and fluff the rice with a fork, and add meat if you would like. Serve hot.

Yield: 6 servings

Culinary Note:

Cold brown rice is also very good the next day to make a cold salad.

DINNER'S READY

TURMERIC RICE

⅓ cup scallions, sliced
1 Tablespoon butter
4 cups water
1 Tablespoon lemon juice
   (or orange juice)
1½ teaspoons instant beef
   bouillon granules

¼ teaspoon salt
¼ teaspoon ground turmeric
2 cups long grain rice
½ cup light raisins

Garnish: fresh parsley

How to Prepare:

1. In a large heavy saucepan with a heavy lid, cook the scallions (sometimes called green onions) in butter until tender.
2. Now add the water, lemon juice, bouillon granules, salt and turmeric. Bring to a full boil. Add the rice.
3. Cover the saucepan and turn down the heat to a simmer. Simmer 25 minutes.
4. After 25 minutes is over, turn off the heat and let the rice sit for 5 minutes without removing the lid.
5. Remove the lid and gently fluff up the rice with a fork and gently stir in the light raisins.

Serve garnished with fresh parsley.

Yield: 6 to 8 servings

Culinary Note:

This dish goes very well with a chicken or a beef curry.

77

Recipe Skill Level   Easy
Suggested Age Level 5 and Up

STEAMED WHITE RICE

Rice is the easiest and most versatile dish to prepare. It is used for pilafs, salads, stuffings, puddings and molds. One-third of the world eats rice as its staple food.

1 cup white rice   **1 Tablespoon butter**
2 cups water   **½ teaspoon salt (optional)**

How to Prepare:

1. In a deep, heavy bottomed pot with a lid, bring 2 cups of water to a boil. Add butter and salt, if desired. Add the rice and stir gently with a fork.
2. Cover with a lid, and bring down the heat to a simmer.
3. Simmer the rice for 20 minutes without removing the lid.
4. After 20 minutes, turn off the heat and let the rice stand for 5 minutes.
5. Remove the lid and fluff-up the rice with a fork and serve.

Yield: 4 to 6 servings

Culinary Note:

White rice has an outer covering which is removed by a process called polishing.

Brown rice is any rice that has been hulled but has not lost its bran. It contains more nutrients, especially vitamin B. This takes longer to cook, about 45 minutes.

Converted rice has been hulled, steamed and dried. Sometimes converted rice can be too pasty.

Italian Arborio rice is thicker and shorter than the American rice. It is available in specialty stores and Italian markets. It is used for risotto, paella and jambalaya. It is especially good for rice pudding.

Wild rice is not a rice at all but a seed harvested along the edges of lakes in Minnesota, Wisconsin and Southern Canada. It has a nutty flavor and is very expensive but well worth the cost. It is sometimes mixed with brown rice.

Baking and Dessert Making

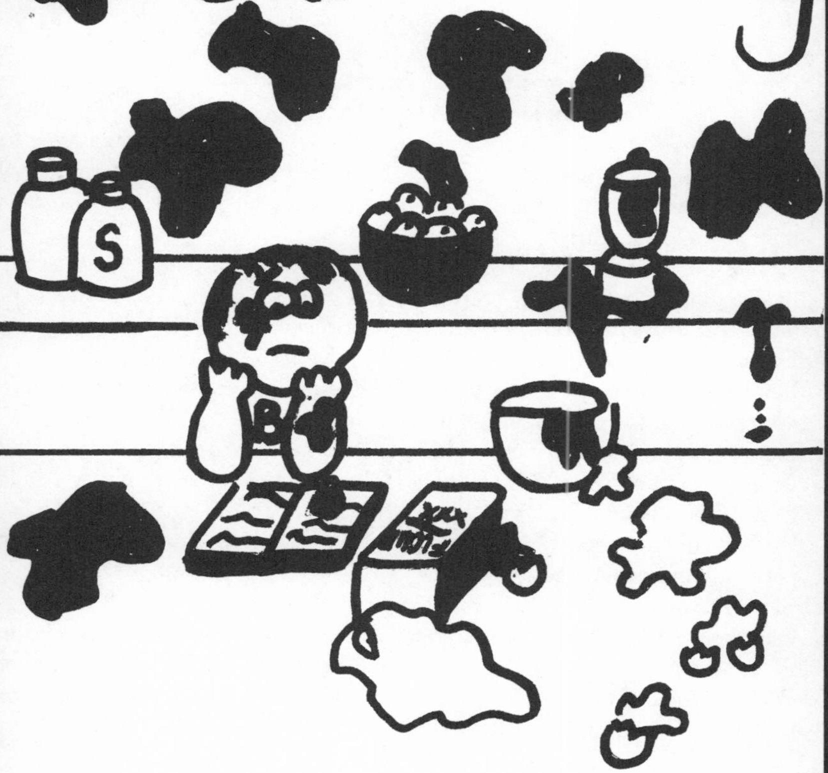

BAKING AND DESSERT MAKING

Recipe Skill Level   Moderate
Suggested Age Level   6 and Up
(With adult assistance.)

BASIC PIE CRUST

1 cup unbleached flour
⅓ cup solid shortening
4 to 5 Tablespoons cold water

Knife and fork
9″ pie pan
Rolling pin
2 sheets waxed paper

How to Prepare:

1. In a medium-sized mixing bowl, add the flour and the shortening.
2. With the knife and the fork, begin to cut the flour and the shortening with a crossing motion.
3. Continue this crossing motion until the mixture is the texture of coarse crumbs.
4. Add the water and mix the dough gently with your fork.
5. Begin to work the dough together with your fingertips. If the dough feels too moist, add a little flour. If the dough is too dry and does not want to hold together, then add a teaspoon of water at a time until you have a consistency that will hold together.
6. Gently work the dough into a ball, then flatten the dough gently into the shape of a flat, fat pancake. If you overwork the dough, it will become tough and not flaky. Try to handle the dough as little as possible.
7. Lay out 2 sheets of waxed paper and sprinkle them with a little flour.
8. Place the dough in the center of one sheet and place the second on top. (The flour will help keep your dough from sticking.)
9. Now gently roll out the dough to form a uniform circle that is a little larger than your 9″ pie pan. You may want to hold the pie pan over the dough as a guide to see if you have the correct size.
10. Remove the top sheet of waxed paper and gently place the dough over your pie plate and center the dough.
11. Slowly remove the top sheet of waxed paper.
12. Gently work the dough into the corners of the pan with your fingertips and crimp the edges of the pie crust with the end of a fork to create a little striped pattern.
13. Prick the pie crust in various spots gently with a fork. In this way the pie crust will not shrink when it is baked.

Basic Pie Crust ...(continued)

NOTE: Your first pie crust is always the most difficult, but if you follow these directions the first time, the second crust should be a breeze. Making a pie crust should be fun, and you will get to know the "feel" of the dough.

Yield: 1 pie crust

Culinary Note:

Unbleached flour is different from all-purpose white flour because it has no chemicals added.

BAKING AND
DESSERT MAKING

Recipe Skill Level   Medium
Suggested Age Level   6 and Up

BRAN AND APRICOT COOKIES

The combination of bran, brown sugar and dried apricots makes a mellow flavored, slightly tart cookie.

1 cup bran bud-type cereal	**½ cup firmly packed brown sugar**
1 cup all-purpose flour	**½ cup granulated sugar**
⅔ cup dried apricots, chopped	**1 large egg**
½ teaspoon baking soda	**1 Tablespoon milk**
½ teaspoon baking powder	**1 Tablespoon vanilla**
½ teaspoon salt	**Solid vegetable shortening**
½ cup butter, softened	**to grease cookie sheet**

How to Prepare:

1. Preheat the oven to 350.°
2. Combine the bran, flour, apricots, baking soda, baking powder and the salt in a large mixing bowl. Set aside.
3. Cream together the butter, brown sugar and the granulated sugar.
4. Now add the eggs, milk and vanilla.
5. Add the bran mixture to the sugar mixture just until the ingredients are evenly mixed. Do not overmix.
6. Grease 2 cookie sheets with solid shortening and drop batter by Tablespoons onto cookie sheets leaving 2" between cookies. These cookies spread.
7. Bake cookies for 10 to 12 minutes or until they are a light golden color.
8. Cool on wire racks.

Yield: Approx. 40 cookies

NOTE: In order to soften butter, simply leave it on the kitchen counter until ready to use, for about 1 hour.

81

CHOCOLATINES

12 ounces semi-sweet chocolate
4 ounces bitter chocolate
2 ounces butter
1 cup sugar
1⅔ cup brown sugar
1½ cups all-purpose flour
½ teaspoon baking powder

4 eggs
1 Tablespoon plus 1 teaspoon
  vanilla
¼ cup water
1 pound chocolate chips
2 cups walnut pieces

How to Prepare:

1. Melt together in a medium-sized saucepan, the 12 ounces of semi-sweet chocolate, bitter chocolate and butter. (Chocolate burns very easily so you may wish to melt the butter in a double boiler, a medium-sized saucepan which is in another larger saucepan filled with simmering water.) Set aside.
2. Combine sugar, brown sugar, flour, baking powder, eggs, vanilla and water.
3. Add this mixture to the chocolate mixture and blend well.
4. Stir in chocolate chips and walnuts and mix well.
5. Drop by large spoonfuls onto cookie sheets covered with parchment paper.
6. Bake for 15 to 20 minutes at 350.° Watch these cookies very carefully. Do not overbake. They should come out like brownies and firm up as they cool.

Yield: Approx. 24 cookies

<u>CARROT BREAD or MUFFINS</u>

¾ cup vegetable oil
2 eggs
1 cup all-purpose flour
1 cup sugar
½ teaspoon baking soda
½ teaspoon baking powder
⅛ teaspoon ginger
½ teaspoon cinnamon
1 cup carrot, shredded
½ cup flaked coconut

½ cup walnut or pecans
(optional)
½ cup raisins (optional)

1 3-ounce package cream
cheese
4 Tablespoons butter
1 cup confectioners sugar
1 teaspoon vanilla

Loaf pan or cupcake tins

How to Prepare:

1. Combine vegetable oil and eggs and blend well.
2. Add flour, sugar, baking soda, baking powder, ginger, cinnamon and mix well.
3. Add shredded carrot (use great care when using a grater that you do not scrape your knuckles while doing this), coconut, walnuts and raisins and blend well.
4. Bake in preheated 350° oven for 45 minutes for a loaf pan and 30 minutes for muffins.
5. When baked, remove to a metal rack and cool.
6. To make the frosting, combine cream cheese, butter, confectioners sugar and vanilla and mix well. This mixes well in a food processor.
7. Frost the loaf or muffins. This recipe is very good even without the icing. Muffins also travel in lunch boxes or trips without the icing.

Yield: Approx. 36 muffins

83

IRISH SODA BREAD

This recipe produces a lovely round biscuit with a brown, flaky crust and the flavor of raisins and caraway seeds. This is fun to make all year long.

Caraway is one of the oldest spices known to man; remains have been found dating from the Neolithic era. In those days, it was used in cooking and particularly in medicine and as a magic plant to chase off evil spirits. The seeds are said to aid in digestion and it is also believed that it stimulates the appetite. Today it grows wild in meadows and pastures throughout Central and Northern Europe, in some Asian regions and in Canada.

**2 cups all-purpose white
   or bread flour
4 teaspoons baking powder
½ teaspoon salt
1 Tablespoon sugar
3 Tablespoons solid vegetable
   shortening**

**Additional solid vegetable
   shortening to grease cake pan
⅔ cup milk
½ cup raisins (add more if
   you would like)
1 Tablespoon caraway seeds
   (optional)**

9″ round cake pan

How to Prepare:

1. Preheat the oven to 375.°
2. Grease a 9″ round cake pan with a little solid vegetable shortening.
3. In a large bowl, put in the flour, baking powder, salt and sugar and work in the shortening with a knife and fork with a cutting motion.
4. Quickly stir the milk into the dough.
5. Now add the raisins and the caraway seeds, stirring just enough to distribute them evenly.
6. Turn the dough out onto a lightly floured surface and knead about 20 times or until the dough holds together nicely. (Young children may need some help with kneading in the beginning.)
7. Place the dough in the cake pan and bake it for 20 to 30 minutes. The timing is different for every oven because no two ovens bake at exactly the same temperature. If you check for doneness between this time, you will be safe.

8. When baked, cool the pan on a metal rack for 10 minutes, then remove the bread with potholders to help the bread cool evenly.
9. Cut the bread into wedges, like a pie, and serve the Irish Soda Bread warm with lots of nice, unsalted butter.

Yield: 1 - 9" round loaf

Culinary Note:

To KNEAD means to work dough by pressing it with the heels of the hands, folding and turning it and pressing it until it has been worked into a contained elastic texture.

BAKING AND DESSERT MAKING

Recipe Skill Level   Easy
Suggested Age Level   5 and Up

CORN BREAD

This recipe is sturdy, solid and slightly dry and is a direct legacy from our American past.

¾ **cup yellow cornmeal**
1 cup all-purpose flour
⅓ **cup sugar**
3 teaspoons baking powder
½ **teaspoon salt (optional)**

1 cup milk
1 egg, well beaten
2 Tablespoons butter or
    shortening, melted

How to Prepare:

1. Preheat the oven to 425.°
2. Grease an 8" square cake pan and set aside.
3. Mix together the cornmeal, flour, sugar, baking powder and salt in a large bowl.
4. Now add the milk, egg and butter and blend well.
5. Spoon this mixture into the pan and bake for about 20 minutes.
6. Cool and cut into squares. This corn bread also tastes great when it is warm from the oven.

Yield: 6 servings

85

APPLE CRISP

Butter to grease the casserole
6 large tart cooking apples
  (Granny Smith are great)
½ small fresh lemon

2 Tablespoons butter
¼ cup sugar
1 teaspoon to 2 teaspoons
  ground cinnamon

Topping

⅔ cup all-purpose flour
⅔ cup sugar

4 Tablespoons butter, softened

Standard size baking dish

How to Prepare:

1. Preheat the oven to 375.° Butter casserole and set aside.
2. Peel, core and slice the apples. Put apple slices in a large mixing bowl and sprinkle them with juice from the lemon. (This will add flavor and also keep the apples from turning color.)
3. Melt 2 Tablespoons butter in a saucepan and pour over the apples.
4. Add ¼ cup sugar and the cinnamon to the apples and toss to mix the ingredients. Put the mixture into a casserole.
5. To make the topping, mix the flour and the sugar together in a small mixing bowl. Add the butter and blend lightly with your fingers to form fine crumbs. Sprinkle the crumbs over the apples in the casserole.
6. Place the casserole in the oven and bake, uncovered, until the apple juice bubbles over onto the browned crusty topping, about 50 to 60 minutes.

Yield: Approx. 6 to 8 servings

"An Apple A Day Keeps the Doctor Away!"

BAKING AND
DESSERT MAKING

Recipe Skill Level   Moderate
Suggested Age Level   10 and Up

PEAR TART

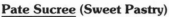

Pate Sucree (Sweet Pastry)

1¾ cups all-purpose flour
6 ounces (1¼ sticks) butter
¼ cup sugar

2 egg yolks
¼ teaspoon water
4 drops vanilla

Filling

½ cup sugar
3 Tablespoons flour
1 egg
3 ounces butter (¾ stick), melted

4 Bartlett pears (peeled and
   sliced in half) *

Garnish: Confectioners sugar

How to Prepare:

1. Preheat the oven to 375.°
2. To prepare the crust, combine the flour, butter and sugar in a food processor and blend several seconds. If you do not have a food processor, blend by hand.
3. Add the yolks, water and vanilla slowly.
4. Test consistency. If the dough fails to hold together, add a few extra drops of water.
5. Remove and roll out the dough with a rolling pin between 2 plastic luncheon bags. The dough will not stick and you do not have to use flour. Hold a tart pan over the dough to make sure your circle is the right size. Remove the plastic.
6. Fit into your tart pan and freeze while you prepare the filling.
7. To prepare the filling, combine the sugar, flour, egg, melted butter and pour half the filling into your tart shell.
8. Score (make small slices across) the pears and place them gently in a circle in the tart shell.
9. Pour the remainder of the filling on top and bake in the preheated oven for 40 to 45 minutes until it is golden brown. (Important: Use a sheet of aluminum foil underneath your tart pan on the rack in the oven. The butter in the crust drips and creates a burning problem in the oven.)
10. Remove from the oven and cool on a rack. When completely cool, sprinkle the tart with confectioners sugar and serve.

Yield: 8 servings

NOTE: Apples also work well in this recipe.

87

PECAN TASSIES

1 stick (½ cup) plus
  1 Tablespoon unsalted butter,
  softened
3 ounces cream cheese,
  softened slightly
1 cup all-purpose flour
1 large egg
¾ cup firmly packed light
  brown sugar

½ cup pecans, chopped
⅛ teaspoon vanilla
Pinch of salt

Special equipment:
miniature cupcake/muffin tins
(available in gourmet shops)

How to Prepare:

1. Preheat oven to 350.°
2. In a bowl, combine one stick of butter and the cream cheese.
3. Stir in the flour and form the dough into a ball.
4. Divide the dough into 24 equal pieces and press the pieces into the bottom and up the sides of 24 small (2 Tablespoons) muffin tins.
5. In a small bowl, beat the egg lightly with the brown sugar and stir in the pecans, the remaining Tablespoon of butter, the vanilla and a pinch of salt.
6. Divide the filling among the pastry-lined tins.
7. Bake the tassies for 25 minutes or until the filling is puffed slightly and the pastry is golden.
8. Let the tassies cool on a wire rack. When cool, gently remove them from the tins and store in an airtight container.

Yield: 24 tassies

Culinary Note:

Nuts are rich in protein, vitamins, calcium, iron and oils. Buy them in small quantities and store them in a cool spot. Pecan is an American Indian word and these were used in tribal cookery. They are used today to enrich cakes, confectionery and ice cream, but their proudest moment comes at Thanksgiving in dark toffee-colored Pecan Pie, a rich, sweet mixture, similar to Pecan Tassies, of syrup, brown sugar, eggs, vanilla and nuts.

CHINESE FORTUNE COOKIES

Flour
3 Tablespoons butter, softened
3 Tablespoons sugar
1 egg white
½ teaspoon vanilla

Fortunes: Use slips of paper to make out special messages for friends or family. Cut these small, about ¼" by 2."

Cookie sheet
3" cookie cutter

How to Prepare:

1. Preheat oven to 400.°
2. Cut out fortunes and fold in half lengthwise, then crosswise and set aside.
3. Grease cookie sheet, dip the rim of a 3" cookie cutter or glass in flour and press 6 outlines firmly 1" apart on prepared sheet. Set aside.
4. In a small bowl, beat butter, sugar, egg white and vanilla until well blended.
5. With a small spatula spread rounded teaspoonful of batter in each outlined circle. Spread sparingly.
6. Bake in oven for 4 to 5 minutes and watch carefully. They are done when the edges are lightly browned.
7. Remove the cookie sheet immediately and quickly loosen the cookie with a spatula.
8. Turn the bottom side up and fold the cookie in the center (HOT - use a paper napkin), then very gently fold the cookie in half after placing the fortune in the center. Hold the edges together for 3 seconds. Grasp the folded ends of the cookie and place the center of the fold over the rim of a glass. Gently press the ends down to bend the cookie in the middle. Cool.
9. If the cookies cool and become too brittle to fold, then return them to the oven briefly to soften.

Yield: Approx. 20 cookies

HAMANTASCHEN
(Haman's Hats)

These lovely tri-cornered pastries are traditionally served at Purim time and are filled with prunes or poppyseeds. Haman was a counselor to King Ashareus, and these little cookies represent the shape of his hat.

These take a little time but are well worth the extra effort. You might like to do them in three steps: STEP #1 - Make the dough; STEP #2 - Make the filling; and STEP #3 - Shape the cookies and bake.

Dough

1 cup sugar
¼ pound butter (1 stick), softened
2 large eggs
1 teaspoon vanilla
4 cups all-purpose flour
1½ teaspoons baking powder
¼ teaspoon salt
Grated lemon or orange rind

Filling

14 oz. package pitted prunes
4 thin slices orange
½ cup walnuts (chopped)
Juice and rind of 1 lemon
6 Tablespoons sugar
1 Tablespoon oil
Dash of nutmeg
Note: The prune filling can always be substituted with a prepared fruit filling if you dislike prunes.

3½" cookie cutter (or you may substitute the top rim of a glass)
2 plastic luncheon-size bags
Rolling pin
Cookie sheet

BAKING AND DESSERT MAKING

<u>HAMANTASCHEN</u> (continued)

<u>How to Prepare</u>:

1. Preheat the oven to 350.°
2. To prepare the dough, cream together the sugar and the softened butter with an electric mixer or by hand in a large bowl using a wooden spoon.
3. Now add the eggs and the vanilla to the mixture.
4. In a separate bowl, mix together the flour, baking powder, salt and the grated lemon (or orange) rind.
5. Keeping the mixer at a slow speed, add the flour mixture.
6. Turn out the dough onto a lightly floured surface to knead gently by hand. If the dough is too moist, flour your hands, and continue kneading until the dough is smooth.
7. Refrigerate the dough one hour wrapped in plastic wrap. This will firm up the dough and make it easier to work with.
8. Remove the dough from the refrigerator and shape into a flat, thick pancake shape with your hands.
9. Using 2 plastic luncheon-size bags, roll out the dough between them to about ⅛″ thickness with the rolling pin.
10. Remove the top sheet of the luncheon bag and cut the dough with a cookie cutter (or glass) into 3½″ rounds. Set aside. Reuse all scraps of dough and reroll as before.
11. To prepare the filling, cook the prunes with the orange slices in a small amount of water until tender. Set aside to cool.
12. In a blender or a food processor, combine the cooled prunes with the rest of the ingredients. Transfer the mixture to a small bowl and set aside.
13. To make your cookies, place a heaping teaspoon of the filling into the center of each dough round and gently draw up 2 sides and the third side across in a triangular form. Pinch the edges together to form a tri-cornered pocket.
14. Bake the cookies on a lightly greased cookie sheet at 350° for approximately 20 minutes. Cool on a wire rack.

Yield: Approx. 45 cookies

Culinary Terms:

(a) To "soften" butter, you simply let the butter sit out on a counter for 1 hour before you are ready to use it.
(b) To "cream" butter and sugar means to work the butter around the inside of a bowl with an electric beater until it is soft and creamy. If you are working by hand, press and beat the butter and sugar with a wooden spoon until it is creamy and blends well together.

**BAKING AND
DESSERT MAKING**

Recipe Skill Level   Moderate
Suggested Age Level   9 and Up
(Child needs adult supervision with
stirring chocolate and dipping
strawberries.)

CHOCOLATE COVERED STRAWBERRIES

The arrival of strawberries heralds the coming of summer, but they will not be full flavored and sweet until late in the season.

Our cultivated strawberry today is a hybrid of a fragrant strawberry from Chile (in South America) crossbred with the Virginia strawberry. It is a true balance of size and taste.

They should be plump and glossy with green frills intact. Watch for any soft or mushy ones that are hidden in the bottom of a pint of strawberries.

Do not wash strawberries until you are ready to use them. Give them a quick rinse under cold running water. If you choose to sugar your strawberries a little before serving, they will give off their natural juices.

1 pint fresh strawberries   **Mini-paper candy cups (optional)**
8 ounces sweet, semi-sweet   **Toothpicks**
**   or milk chocolate, chopped**   **Waxed paper**

How to Prepare:

1. Gently wash and hull one pint of fresh strawberries.
2. Drain the strawberries thoroughly on paper towels or in a colander. (Melted chocolate will not adhere or stick to a wet strawberry.)
3. Melt the 8 ounces of chocolate in a *double-boiler and stir gently until just melted. Let the chocolate cool just a bit.
4. Using a toothpick, dip the strawberries in the chocolate briefly, covering two-thirds of the strawberry on all sides. Leave some of the beautiful color showing.
5. Cool the chocolate-dipped strawberries on waxed paper or aluminum foil.
6. Refrigerate the strawberries only until the chocolate sets. Remove them from the refrigerator and store them in a cool spot, covered, until you are ready to serve them. (These are very perishable and should not be held for more than 24 hours. If they are kept in the refrigerator too long, when they are removed the chocolate sweats and is too hard and the strawberry gets soft.)

Get Dipped Here

Serving Suggestion: Place them in tiny paper candy cups and serve them on your prettiest plate. They make lovely gifts. Something you make yourself is always very special.

*If you don't have a DOUBLE BOILER, use a small saucepan to melt your chocolate and place it inside another larger pot which has a little water in it before you place it on the stove. In this way, the chocolate will not burn. Burned chocolate must be thrown away because it becomes very bitter.

Yield: Approx. 12 to 14

BAKING AND DESSERT MAKING

Recipe Skill Level   Easy
Suggested Age Level   8 and Up

OLD FASHIONED LEMON BARS

Crust:

½ cup butter, softened   **¼ cup sugar**
1⅓ cups all-purpose flour

Filling:

2 eggs   **¼ teaspoon baking powder**
½ cup sugar   **3 teaspoons fresh lemon juice**
2 Tablespoons all-purpose flour

Confectioners sugar

How to Prepare:

1. Preheat oven to 350.°
2. In medium-sized mixing bowl of the electric mixer, combine crust ingredients and mix on low speed until blended, about 1 minute.
3. Pat into an ungreased 8″ square baking pan and bake near the center of the oven for 15 to 20 minutes or until brown on the edges. Remove from the oven and set aside.
4. To make the filling, combine all the filling ingredients and blend well.
5. Pour the filling ingredients over the partially baked crust.
6. Return the batter to the oven and bake for 18 to 20 minutes or until set.
7. Remove from the oven.
8. When cool, sprinkle with confectioners sugar.

Yield: 16 bars

Recipe Skill Level   Moderate
Suggested Age Level   10 and Up

CREAM PUFFS
(Paté a Chou)

1 cup water
¾ teaspoon salt
½ cup butter
1 cup all-purpose flour

4 to 5 eggs
1 cup heavy cream
¼ cup confectioners sugar
1 teaspoon vanilla

Pastry bag (optional)

How to Prepare:

1. Preheat the oven to 400.°
2. In a small saucepan, heat the water, salt and butter until the butter is melted.
3. Heat to a boil. Remove from stove to a heat-proof surface.
4. Add all the flour at once and quickly stir with a wooden spoon until the mixture is smooth and pulls away from the pan to form a ball.
5. Put the pan back on a low flame and beat the dough for 30 seconds to one minute to dry the mixture. Remove the pan from the heat and cool slightly.
6. Beat into the mixture 1 egg at a time, completely mixing each before adding the next. The consistency of the dough should be very shiny and just falls from a spoon. You may need to add only part of the fifth egg to the dough.
7. Shape cream puffs using a pastry bag and a star tip. Make all the puffs the same size so they will all be done in the oven at the same time. You should have 2 lightly greased cookie sheets available. (If you do not have a pastry bag, you may simply drop a Tablespoon of dough at a time onto the cookie sheet.) Puffs will double in size so leave space between them.
8. Put the puffs in the oven and bake for 25 to 30 minutes until firm and brown.
9. Open the oven door and make a small slit in each puff with the tip of a sharp knife. Prop the oven door open with a wooden spoon and let the puffs sit in the oven (with heat turned off) for about 15 minutes to dry out.
10. Remove the puffs and let cool to room temperature.
11. Slice the cream puffs in half horizontally and pull out the uncooked center portion.
12. Fill the center with fresh whipped cream and sprinkle confectioners sugar on the top with a sifter.

NOTE: You can also fill the cream puff shells with ice cream or pudding or fresh fruit. These are also fun to fill with egg or tuna salad when friends come over to visit.

FRESH WHIPPED CREAM: In an electric mixer, whip 1 cup of heavy cream until almost stiff. Slowly add ¼ cup confectioners sugar and 1 teaspoon vanilla.

Yield: 12

Chocolate Delights

CHOCOLATE DELIGHTS

THE STORY OF CHOCOLATE
or
MONEY GROWS ON TREES

Money grows on trees. At least it did in Aztec times. The "tree" is the cocoa tree which grows near the equator. Archeologists suggest that cocoa was cultivated first by the Mayans who took it with them when they migrated to the Yucatan in about the 6th century A.D. The Aztecs carried the cocoa seeds with them as they wandered through Central America — using them as money.

Clearly this cocoa bean was special. According to several historical accounts, chocolate was used as a special "toast." Legend tells us that this chocolate was an intoxicating drink. One supposes that the Indians mixed their ground cocoa beans with fermented corn mash instead of with water to achieve this effect.

Chocolate, the essence of the cocoa bean, is even said to have mythological and religious roots. The Indians believed that the Aztec god Quetzalcoatl brought the seeds of the cocoa tree from the "Garden of Life" and gave them to man.

Many early explorers experienced chocolate on their travels. Christopher Columbus was given a chocolate drink by the Mexican Indians but he wasn't impressed. The explorer Cortez was toasted with chocolate at the Aztec court. He was impressed and he established a cocoa plantation under the Spanish flag to grow "money" for the king.

Chocolate — The Fun Food

We all know that chocolate is a fun food but did you know that it is also a nutritious food? Chocolate is a high energy food which contains protein, carbohydrate, and fat. In addition, it contains calcium, phosphorus, iron, sodium, potassium, vitamin A and some B vitamins. However, eaten in large quantities, chocolate can be bad for the teeth and figure. Eaten in moderation it is a joy to the spirit.

Real Chocolate

Real chocolate begins with chocolate liqueur and cocoa butter. Basically there are two kinds of real chocolate, unsweetened and sweetened.

Unsweetened chocolate: When the cocoa beans are cleaned, dried, roasted and ground to a paste, a chocolate liqueur remains. To make chocolate, cocoa butter, obtained by pressing beans, is added in varying amounts. The "liqueur" is solidified and molded to become the unsweetened chocolate you use in recipes. When this is powdered, it is the cocoa powder.

96

Chocolate Story (continued)

Sweetened chocolate: When sugar and cocoa butter are added to chocolate liqueur, it becomes sweetened chocolate. The addition of milk produces milk chocolate. Clearly, there are a great variety of sweetened chocolates ranging from very sweet to bitter sweet. White chocolate, however, is pure cocoa butter with the addition of sugar, milk and flavorings.

Imitation Chocolate

Generally, the use of cocoa in place of chocolate liqueur and any type of vegetable fat substituted for cocoa butter will produce an imitation chocolate. This is called compound chocolate. It is frequently used as an outside coating for chocolates and for chocolate decorations. Compound chocolate also comes in different colors. It is a very popular type of chocolate with bakers because it needs only to be melted to be used and does not discolor when hardened. Real chocolate is much more fragile. In fact, another name for compound chocolate is "summer coating," named because it has a higher melting point.

Carob

Carob is a powder made from the mashed fruit of the carob tree. It too is combined with fats and flavorings to produce a candy-like chocolate. It is no more natural than chocolate. It also has lots of calories and is often selected by people who may be allergic to chocolate. There are other products on the market which contain all synthetic ingredients. Be sure to read your labels.

Cooking with Chocolate

Real chocolate is very fragile and changes consistency when exposed to extremes of heat or when water is added. Therefore, a few special rules are in order to insure your success:

1. Never add water to melting chocolate. Water will cause the chocolate to stiffen and your batch will be ruined. If necessary, you can thin melting chocolate with a teaspoon or two of vegetable oil.
2. Chop chocolate into small pieces for melting. Chocolate will keep its shape even when melted so it should be stirred gently.

Melting Chocolate

1. Place chopped chocolate in the top of an uncovered double boiler. Put the pan over hot but not boiling water. On low heat, stir until the chocolate is melted and smooth. It is best not to cover your pan because droplets of water can form inside the lid and drip into your chocolate mixture. Or...
2. Melt chocolate in a microwave oven. Place chocolate in microwave container and heat for 1 to 2 minutes. Stir until smooth.

Chocolate Story (continued)

3. Refrigerate your finished real chocolate items for a few hours before serving time.

   Real chocolate is always tempered by candy makers before it is used for coating candy or it will discolor when it hardens. Tempering is a complex process which can be avoided in your kitchen. Since you probably aren't making enormous quantities of chocolates, you can have beautiful looking chocolates by simply refrigerating them for a few hours.

4. Store your chocolates in a cool place. When chocolate, even tempered chocolate, is kept at high temperatures or in the sun, the cocoa butter will begin to melt and the surface of chocolate will become grey. This change is called "bloom." The taste doesn't change, however, but the chocolates look aged and unattractive.

CHOCOLATE DELIGHTS

Recipe Skill Level   Moderate
Suggested Age Level   10 and Up

ACORNS

20 dried apricots (approximately)   **⅓ cup ground pecans or**
6 ounces chocolate, chopped   **hazelnuts (optional)**

How to Prepare:

1. Melt the chocolate in the top of a double boiler over barely simmering water. Stir gently until melted.
2. To dip the apricots, hold the apricots at the broad end and dip them into the chocolate mixture only halfway.
3. Hold over the pan and let the excess drain off. The chocolate will drain to a point.
4. If desired, wait a few minutes and then dip the tip carefully into ground pecans or hazelnuts.
5. Place the acorns on parchment paper to harden.

Serving Suggestion:

Place the acorns in small, individual paper cups.

Yield: 24 acorns

CHOCOLATE DELIGHTS

Recipe Skill Level   Moderate
Suggested Age Level   10 and Up

ANDREA'S FUDGE CAKE

This is said to be the fudgiest chocolate cake ever! Stencil your own decoration.

12 ounces semi-sweet chocolate (chopped)
5 Tablespoons expresso or strong coffee
1 cup butter
2 cups sugar
6 egg yolks

1 cup all-purpose flour
6 egg whites

9" spring form pan with removable bottom
1 paper lace doily for stenciling
¼ cup produced confectioners sugar

How to Prepare:

1. Preheat the oven to 350.° Grease and lightly sugar a 9" spring form pan. Use sugar instead of flour to prepare your pan for a tastier edge.
2. Melt the semi-sweet, chopped chocolate with expresso or strong coffee in a double boiler. Stir gently until melted and remove the pan from the heat. Cool the mixture for about 15 minutes or until it reaches room temperature.
3. Beat the butter until creamy and add the sugar. Beat until fluffy.
4. Add the egg yolks, one at a time, to the butter and sugar mixture.
5. Add the flour and set aside.
6. In a separate bowl, beat the egg whites until stiff. Be sure the bowl and beater are clean, or the egg whites will not stiffen.
7. Pour the cooled chocolate mixture into the egg whites. Fold gently with a rubber spatula.
8. Fold the chocolate/egg white mixture into the butter/egg/flour mixture just until combined.
9. Pour the batter into the prepared pan. Bake 60 to 70 minutes at 350.° When the cake is done, the top will look crusty and cracked. The center will be slightly moist and fudgy. Do not overbake.
10. To decorate the cake, stencil with powdered sugar. When the cake is completely cooled, place paper lace doily onto the top of the cake. Gently shake the powdered sugar through a strainer onto the doily. Carefully lift doily and your stencil decoration remains. You might be very clever and make your own stencil. It is not necessary to frost this cake unless you want to.
11. Garnish your stenciled cake with chocolate leaves or curls (see recipe in this book) or a perfect strawberry on the plate beside the slice of cake.

Culinary Note:

See page 40 for instructions on separating eggs.

99

CHOCOLATE DELIGHTS   Recipe Skill Level   Difficult
                        Suggested Age Level   10 and Up

CHOCOLATE LEAVES

Chocolate leaves make a super decoration on top of cakes or on ice cream. Imagine them on a dish of fresh strawberries or raspberries and cream.

2 ounces bittersweet chocolate

Fresh green leaves (gardenia, ivy or rose leaves)
Clean artist's paint brush (keep one just for chocolate)

How to Prepare:

1. Separate the leaves but keep enough stem on each so you can grasp it. Wash leaves and pat dry with paper towels.
2. Melt chopped chocolate in the top of a double boiler over barely simmering water. Stir the chocolate until melted and smooth.
3. Hold the leaf upside down in your left hand. Paint an even layer of melted chocolate over the veined (underside) of the leaf. Be careful not to let the chocolate run onto the front of the leaf.
4. Place the leaf, chocolate side up, on a small plate in the refrigerator or freezer just until the chocolate is set, about 5 minutes.
5. Gently and carefully peel away the green leaf starting at the stem end. Handle the chocolate as little as possible because the heat from your hand will cause the chocolate to melt.
6. Keep the finished chocolate leaves stored in the refrigerator or freezer until needed.
7. To make the chocolate leaves shiny, you can paint them with a light coating of vegetable oil or spray them with a canned vegetable oil product.

CHOCOLATE DELIGHTS

Recipe Skill Level   Moderate
Suggested Age Level   10 and Up

CHOCOLATE CURLS

These are a nifty decoration for cakes and ice cream.

3 ounces semi-sweet, milk or white chocolate, chopped

Waxed paper or parchment paper
2 clean cake pans
Metal spatula

How to Prepare:

1. Melt the chocolate in the top of a double boiler over barely simmering water. Stir until smooth.
2. Turn the cake pans upside down. Using a spatula, spread the melted chocolate in a thin layer on the bottom outside surface of the upside down cake pan.
3. Chill the chocolate coated pan for 10 to 15 minutes in the refrigerator.
4. Remove one pan at a time from the refrigerator. Put the metal spatula under an edge of chocolate and push it firmly away so that the chocolate curls.
5. Place the curls directly on waxed paper and chill them as they are made. If the chocolate becomes too soft, chill the pan again.
6. Refrigerate or freeze them until you are ready to use them. These decorations are best made on a clear, dry day. The chocolate will harden quickly.

CHOCOLATE DELIGHTS

Recipe Skill Level   Moderate
Suggested Age Level   10 and Up

CHOCOLATE DIPPED PRETZELS

You can also use this recipe for potato chips.

Pretzels
Potato chips
6 ounces of chocolate of your choice, chopped

Parchment paper

How to Prepare:

1. Melt the chocolate in the top of a double boiler over simmering water until melted. Stir gently.
2. Grasp the pretzel at the top and dip it into the melted chocolate so that about three-fourths of the pretzel is covered with chocolate.
3. Let the excess chocolate drip back into the pan.
4. Place the pretzel on parchment paper to allow the chocolate to harden.

NOTE: Follow the same directions for coating potato chips in chocolate.

CHOCOLATE DELIGHTS

Recipe Skill Level   Moderate
Suggested Age Level   10 and Up

CAROB ALMOND RINGS

¼ cup plus 1 Tablespoon
  unsalted butter
1½ Tablespoons light honey
¼ cup blanched almonds,
  ground

1 cup sifted whole wheat
  pastry flour
1½ Tablespoons carob powder
1 teaspoon vanilla

How to Prepare:

1. Preheat the oven to 300.°
2. Beat the butter in a large bowl of the electric mixer until light and creamy.
3. Add the honey and mix well.
4. Add the almonds and beat again.
5. Stir in the whole wheat pastry flour, carob powder and the vanilla with a wooden spoon.
6. Lightly flour the baking sheet.
7. Roll small handful of dough between the palms to form a sausage shape. Transfer this to a work surface and use the hands to roll the dough into larger cylinder about ⅜" thick.
8. Cut this into 3" pieces. Join the ends together to form rings, carefully pressing the ends together to seal. Repeat with the remaining dough.
9. Bake the cookies for 20 to 25 minutes. Cool on wire racks. Store in airtight container.

Yield: 36 cookies

NOTE: Instead of rings, why not form your initials?

Treats For Our Pets

Recipe Skill Level   Easy
Suggested Age Level 5 and Up

DIET FOR NEWBORN MAMMALS

This recipe is not really appropriate for household pets, unless of course, you live in the country and find a baby raccoon in the woods. Never approach a mother or father raccoon, because they can be very nasty.

This formula is what the Zoo baby mammals are fed who are rejected by their mothers. The recipe was contributed by Ann Hess of the Veterinary Department at the Philadelphia Zoological Gardens which is America's first zoo.

There are different types of milk formulas fed to various animals at the Philadelphia Zoo, but this is the one they use the most.

2 ounces evaporated milk
2 ounces water
4 ounce baby bottle with nipple

How to Prepare:

1. In a 4 ounce baby bottle, combine the milk and water and shake well.
2. The formula should either be at room temperature or warm it slightly by running the bottle under hot running water.

NOTE: The best way to test the temperature for baby's milk, whether human or animal, is to apply a few drops of milk to your wrist to see if it's too hot. If it is, let it sit for a few minutes and test again.

Nutritional Note:

The Philadelphia Zoo also adds a liquid multiple vitamin and iron supplement that is made for human infants. A few animals have an intolerance to lactose in milk, so they add something called "Lactaid" to the can of milk which breaks down the lactose making the milk easier to digest.

Recipe Skill Level   Moderate
Suggested Age Level   10 and Up

OATMEAL PEANUT BUTTER DOG BISCUITS

3 cups whole wheat flour
1½ cups 40% bran cereal
½ cup quick-cooking oatmeal
1 teaspoon salt
½ cup safflower oil
2 eggs, lightly beaten
1 cup milk
½ cup peanut butter
¼ cup honey

Waxed paper
Rolling pin
Cookie cutters (gourmet shops
carry bone-shaped cookie
cutters)
Solid vegetable shortening
Cookie sheet
Flour (for dusting waxed paper)

How to Prepare:

1. Preheat the oven to 350.°
2. Using a paper towel, lightly grease a cookie sheet and set aside.
3. In a mixing bowl, combine the dry ingredients which include the whole wheat flour, the bran cereal, the oatmeal and the salt.
4. Stir in the oil, eggs, milk, peanut butter and the honey.
5. Form the dough into a ball, then gently flatten the dough into a fat pancake shape. (This makes rolling the dough easier with less tearing on the ends.)
6. Roll out the dough between 2 pieces of waxed paper which has been floured lightly. Remove 1 sheet of the waxed paper.
7. Using your cookie cutter, cut out biscuits the size suitable for your pet. Your dog might enjoy biscuits in the shape of people or squirrels, rabbits or cats, so look in your cupboard for odd shaped cookie cutters.
8. Place the biscuits on the prepared cookie sheet and bake for about 20 minutes or until done.

Yield: Approx. 48

Recipe courtesy of Ned Moser, M.S., V.M.D., Resident in Clinical Nutrition at the University of Pennsylvania, School of Veterinary Medicine.

TREATS FOR OUR PETS

Recipe Skill Level   Easy
Suggested Age Level   12 and Up
(Note: Caution should be used when working with knives and the oven in this recipe, although young children can help prep the marinade.)

KITTY JERKY

1 pound lean beef or lamb

Marinade:

¼ cup salad oil	**1 Tablespoon brown sugar**
½ cup soy sauce	**Salt**
1 large clove garlic, crushed	**Pepper**

How to Prepare:

1. Preheat the oven to 175.°
2. With a knife, remove any excess fat and slice the meat diagonally across the grain into strips ⅛" or ¼" thick. Set aside.
3. To prepare the marinade, combine the salad oil, soy sauce, garlic and brown sugar in a glass bowl.
4. Place the meat in the marinade and leave the meat to marinate for 2 hours or more.
5. Remove the meat from the marinade and sprinkle lightly with salt and pepper. (Remember to be light on the salt because soy sauce has a lot of salt or sodium.)
6. Place the meat strips in the oven on a wire rack over a drip pan which has been placed beneath to catch juices.
7. Leave the oven door ajar by placing a wooden spoon between the oven and the door to keep it slightly open.
8. Dry the strips in the oven in this manner for approximately 5 hours.
9. Remove the Kitty Jerky when it is dry and still flexible and not brittle.
10. Cool and store the Jerky in an airtight container in a cool, dry place.

Culinary Note:

To marinate meat means to place the meat in a liquid in order to tenderize and flavor. The liquid must contain some type of acid such as soy sauce, lemon or lime juice, vinegar, yogurt or even pulped tomatoes. All these acids help to break down connective tissue. Oil is used in many marinades to add succulence. Pounding or cutting is another way to break up connective tissue when using a tougher cut of meat. Lots of flavoring should be added such as herbs, onions, garlic or fresh ginger.

Recipe courtesy of Ned Moser, M.S., V.M.D., Resident in Clinical Nutrition at the University of Pennsylvania, School of Veterinary Medicine.

TREATS FOR OUR PETS   Recipe Skill Level   Easy
                          Suggested Age Level   6 and Up

"SOMETHING IS FISHY" FISH TREAT (FOR FISH)

1 package unflavored gelatin   **⅛ cup dry cat food**
2 sardines, canned   **½ cup boiling water**
Vitamin C tablet   **1 ice cube tray**
  (crushed between two spoons)

How to Prepare:

1. Put all the above ingredients in the blender.
2. Pour ½ cup boiling water over the ingredients and blend.
3. Pour the ingredients into an ice cube tray.
4. Put in the freezer.
5. Take out a cube when you are ready to feed your fish.
6. Use a grater (be careful) on the ice cube over the fish bowl. They will look like little worms but the fish will love it!

Recipe courtesy of Dr. Sheldon L. Gerstenfeld, V.M.D. of Chestnut Hill, Pa.

PARROT SALAD

(for parakeets, cockatiels or the larger parrots)

½ cup plain yogurt
½ cup fresh fruit

Optional: Shredded carrots or broccoli tops

How to Prepare:

1. Mix plain yogurt with any fruit in season.
2. You can also add shredded carrots if you would like or broccoli tops.
3. Important: Do not let this remain in the cage bowl for more than 2 hours.

This delight will give your bird something to "crow about."

Yield: 1 cup

Recipe courtesy of Dr. Sheldon L. Gerstenfeld, V.M.D. of Chestnut Hill, Pa.

TREATS FOR OUR PETS   Recipe Skill Level   Easy
Suggested Age Level   4 and Up

FURRY-GOOD TREATS

(For gerbils and hamsters)

½ cup Grapenuts cereal
½ cup Cheerios
½ cup corn flakes
⅛ cup wheat germ
⅛ cup peanuts

⅛ cup sunflower seeds
  (with shells)
⅛ cup raisins
2 multivitamins (crushed
  between two spoons)

How to Prepare:

1. Combine the above ingredients in a large plastic bag and secure tightly.
2. Shake well.
3. Feed approximately ¼ cup per day per animal. These amounts may vary depending on the size, age and physiological status of the animal.

NOTE: *Small pieces of carrots and apple may be offered as treats. A constant supply of clean water should be available for the animal. This recipe can be adapted for a guinea pig by adding a source of vitamin C.*

Yield: 2 cups

Recipe courtesy of Barbara Toddes, Animal Nutritionist from the Commissary at the Philadelphia Zoo.

115

117

ORDER BLANKS

To order additional copies for friends or relatives of "The Little Gourmet Cookbook for Children," please fill in the coupon below.

Mail to: The Auxiliary of The Children's Hospital of Philadelphia
"The Little Gourmet Cookbook for Children"
One Children's Center
34th Street and Civic Center Boulevard
Philadelphia, PA 19104

Please send me _____ copies of "The Little Gourmet" at $8.95 per copy plus $1.50 per book for postage and handling.

My check or money order is enclosed for $ _____ .

Name _____

Address _____

City _____ State _____ Zip _____

MAKE CHECKS PAYABLE TO: The Auxiliary of The Children's Hospital of Philadelphia.

Mail to: The Auxiliary of The Children's Hospital of Philadelphia
"The Little Gourmet Cookbook for Children"
One Children's Center
34th Street and Civic Center Boulevard
Philadelphia, PA 19104

Please send me _____ copies of "The Little Gourmet" at $8.95 per copy plus $1.50 per book for postage and handling.

My check or money order is enclosed for $ _____ .

Name _____

Address _____

City _____ State _____ Zip _____

MAKE CHECKS PAYABLE TO: The Auxiliary of The Children's Hospital of Philadelphia.

ORDER BLANKS

To order additional copies for friends or relatives of "The Little Gourmet Cookbook for Children," please fill in the coupon below.

Mail to: The Auxiliary of The Children's Hospital of Philadelphia
            "The Little Gourmet Cookbook for Children"
            One Children's Center
            34th Street and Civic Center Boulevard
            Philadelphia, PA 19104

Please send me _____ copies of "The Little Gourmet" at $8.95 per copy plus $1.50 per book for postage and handling.

My check or money order is enclosed for $ _____ .

Name _____

Address _____

City _____ State _____ Zip _____

MAKE CHECKS PAYABLE TO: The Auxiliary of The Children's Hospital of Philadelphia.

Mail to: The Auxiliary of The Children's Hospital of Philadelphia
            "The Little Gourmet Cookbook for Children"
            One Children's Center
            34th Street and Civic Center Boulevard
            Philadelphia, PA 19104

Please send me _____ copies of "The Little Gourmet" at $8.95 per copy plus $1.50 per book for postage and handling.

My check or money order is enclosed for $ _____ .

Name _____

Address _____

City _____ State _____ Zip _____

MAKE CHECKS PAYABLE TO: The Auxiliary of The Children's Hospital of Philadelphia.

Reorder Additional Copies